Communications
in Computer and Information Science 423

John N. Gathegi   Yaşar Tonta
Serap Kurbanoğlu   Umut Al
Zehra Taşkın (Eds.)

Challenges of Information Management Beyond the Cloud

4th International Symposium
on Information Management in a Changing World
IMCW 2013
Limerick, Ireland, September 4-6, 2013
Revised Selected Papers

 Springer

Volume Editors

John N. Gathegi
Yaşar Tonta
Serap Kurbanoğlu
Umut Al
Zehra Taşkın
Hacettepe University, Ankara, Turkey
E-mail: {jgathegi, tonta, serap, umutal, ztaskin}@hacettepe.edu.tr

ISSN 1865-0929   e-ISSN 1865-0937
ISBN 978-3-662-44411-5   e-ISBN 978-3-662-44412-2
DOI 10.1007/978-3-662-44412-2
Springer Heidelberg New York Dordrecht London

Library of Congress Control Number: 2014955001

Typesetting: Camera-ready by author, data conversion by Scientific Publishing Services, Chennai, India

Printed on acid-free paper

Springer is part of Springer Science+Business Media (www.springer.com)

Preface

Cloud computing has transformed the ways in which both individuals and enterprises make use of information technologies (IT) services and network infrastructure within the last decade. Everything including infrastructure, platforms, applications, software, data, and communication is now seen as a "service." Information, the life blood of scientific progress, economic growth, and social development, is mostly produced, disseminated, used, shared, and re-used in digital formats today. Science, industry and business enterprises tend to become "information" enterprises in that even "money" as matter gets converted to "bits" so as to be stored digitally in computers and transmitted as "information" over the network. Enterprises have tended to spend well over 70% of their time and money to support the IT and network infrastructure. Now they embrace cloud-based services to manage information more efficiently and effectively. As information managers we must now look beyond the cloud, collaborate in order to innovate, and inspire while trying to predict what the future holds.

The 4th International Symposium on Information Management in a Changing World (IMCW 2013) co-organized by Hacettepe University Department of Information Management, Turkey, and Limerick Institute of Technology, Ireland, took place in Limerick, Ireland, during September 4-6, 2013. The theme of the symposium was "Beyond the Cloud: Information... Innovation... Collaboration...." With this theme, the symposium aimed to bring together information professionals, computer and information scientists, business people, and engineers to discuss the implications of cloud computing on information management and to contemplate on how to design and develop innovative and collaborative information services beyond the cloud. More than 20 papers were submitted. In addition, 11 papers were submitted with three panel proposals, seven of which specifically deal with intellectual property issues and collaboration in the cloud. All papers, panel and workshop proposals were subjected to a double-blind reviewing process and 11 papers were selected for inclusion in this book along with three keynote papers. The accepted contributions come from seven countries (Belgium, Canada, China, Japan, Turkey, USA, and Venezuela) and address a number of issues dealing with, among others, cloud computing, intellectual property rights in the cloud, information policy, and information security, all in the context of information management.

We would like to take this opportunity to thank both Hacettepe University and Limerick Institute of Technology for their support. It is a great pleasure to thank the symposium keynote speakers Clifford Lynch (Executive Director, Coalition for Networked Information), Christian Verstraete (Chief Technologist, Cloud Strategy Team, Hewlett-Packard), and Marshall Breeding (Independent Consultant). We would also like to thank and acknowledge the hard work of the members of the international Organizing and Program Committees and the Local Committee who invested their time generously to make this event happen.

July 2014   Yaşar Tonta

Organization

The 4th International Symposium on Information Management in a Changing World, (IMCW 2013) was co-organized by Hacettepe University, Department of Information Management, Turkey, and Limerick Institute of Technology, Ireland.

Organizing Committee

Yaşar Tonta	Hacettepe University, Turkey, (Chair)
Umut Al	Hacettepe University, Turkey
Jerald Cavanagh	Limerick Institute of Technology, Ireland
Padraig Kirby	Limerick Institute of Technology, Ireland
Serap Kurbanoğlu	Hacettepe University, Turkey
Mícheál Mac an Airchinnigh	University of Dublin, Trinity College, Ireland
Orçun Madran	Atılım University, Turkey

Program Committee

Serap Kurbanoğlu	Hacettepe University, Turkey, (Chair)
Umut Al	Hacettepe University, Turkey
Ágnes Hajdu Barát	University of Szeged, Hungary
Carla Basili	Sapienza University, Rome, Italy
Albert K. Boekhorst	The Netherlands
Joumana Boustany	Paris Descartes University, France
Fazlı Can	Bilkent University, Turkey
Jerald Cavanagh	Limerick Institute of Technology, Ireland
Leslie Chan	University of Toronto, Canada
John Crawford	Independent Information Professional
Gülçin Cribb	Singapore Management University, Singapore
Kürşat Çağıltay	METU, Turkey
Armando Malheiro da Silva	University of Porto, Portugal
Milena Dobreva	University of Malta, Malta
Dan Dorner	Victoria University of Wellington, New Zealand
Susana Finquelievich	University of Buenos Aires, Argentina
Maria Francisca Abad García	Valencia University, Spain
Nieves González Fernández-Villavicencio	Pablo de Olavide University, Spain
Ayşe Göker	City University London, UK
Chris Hagar	San Jose State University, USA

Local Committee

Jerald Cavanagh   Limerick Institute of Technology, Ireland,
                         (Co-chair)
Padraig Kirby   Limerick Institute of Technology, Ireland,
                         (Co-chair)

Sponsors

Hacettepe University

Limerick Institute of Technology

Springer

Meet in Ireland

Tourist Board Failte Ireland

Innovative Interfaces

CITAVI

Table of Contents

Cloud Architectures and Cultural Memory

Clifford Lynch

Executive Director, Coalition for Networked Information (CNI),
21 Dupont Circle, Suite 800, Washington, DC, 20036, USA
cliff@cni.org

Abstract. The emergence of cloud-based architectures and information services are changing the nature and contents of our cultural record, and simultaneously altering the framework within which our memory organizations can manage and provide access to this record. Of course, many of these issues are not unique to memory organizations but are echoed across all types of government or corporate settings where substantial data and information resources are made available to the public.

In this talk, I explore some of the challenges of provisioning various types of access and use of cultural materials, and ways in which cloud storage and computational utilities interact with these challenges. Current debates about issues such as how to effectively implement emerging national policies about open access to data and publications resulting from government funding within the scholarly world offer interesting case studies of some of these issues. I will look at some of the potential roles of storage clouds and computational clouds as infrastructure for memory organizations. These developments are coupled in ways that are more complex than generally recognized today: the patterns of connectivity and peering among underlying networks establish new borders and privileged pathways for the various groups who want to make use of computationally intensive tools to analyze cultural materials. National consumer broadband policy and deployment are also significant factors in access to these resources; telecommunications and networking market evolution and market failures may require libraries to take on new or expanded roles in facilitating access. I also briefly examine a few of the developments that are reshaping cultural memory and our ability to capture and preserve it, such as the recent attempt to migrate from desktop software to software as a cloud service in both consumer and commercial marketplaces, and the continued evolution of social media platforms.

Keywords: Cloud computing, cloud architectures, cultural memory institutions.

1   Introduction

It is a pleasure to be here and to have an opportunity to open this conference and to reflect on some of the themes that I think will be explored in depth over the next

J.N. Gathegi et al. (Eds.): IMCW 2013, CCIS 423, pp. 1–13, 2014.

couple of days.[1] I am going to give you several perspectives at a high level but I am hopeful that you will see parts of this echoing through the discussions as the conference proceeds.

Let me get on to my main two themes here. First I want to spend a little time clarifying the various ideas covered by "clouds."

2   Clouds and Cloud Services: Working Definitions and Examples

Clouds, of course, have been all the rage in the information technology and even the popular press, among the consultants and technology pundits, and everywhere else for about three, four years now. It's getting to the point where you would be wise to cross-examine anyone who makes reference to "the cloud" fairly carefully because it means totally different things to different people. It has some fairly precise, technical meanings although they range quite broadly: you see *storage clouds*, which are in fairly widespread deployment now, although even there I think the hype about them perhaps outruns the reality. You see *compute* (often used as *compute on demand) clouds*; those are also relatively commonplace, although perhaps more concentrated in certain niche markets than one might think. One of the things that's wonderful about the world of compute clouds, for example, is that you don't have to spend a lot of money up front. So if you are planning to do an Internet startup, and you do not happen to have the money to make capital investments in huge amounts of server capacity for the great success that you are expecting as soon as your service launches, you can use a cloud-based on demand computing service to make capacity planning and provisioning someone else's problem; you will pay a premium for this, but for the many start-up entrepreneurs there is real value here, and we have seen this used extensively by the last generation of such start-ups.

We also are seeing more recently the notion of *service* or *applications* clouds as increasingly ubiquitous environments for doing work, for collaborating or socializing; sometimes we talk about this using terms like *Software as a Service*. This started probably most heavily in the consumer market place where you think of various image sharing services – Tumblr, Flickr, etc. – out there in the cloud. You think of something like Facebook (or Google+) or Twitter as this cloud-based service and yet, as you look at these different services, they increasingly have tendrils everywhere, some of which are visible: you know you will buy something someplace and it will immediately offer you a button to post down on Facebook. In other cases the tendrils and connections are more subterranean, with various brokerage and tracking services gathering up, handing off, or collecting cookies and other tracking implements

---

[1] Note: This is a moderately edited transcript of a keynote address given at the 4th International Symposium on Information Management in a Changing World (IMCW), Limerick, Republic of Ireland on September 4, 2013; it clarifies a few additional points, but retains the character of a talk rather than a formal paper. My thanks to Diane Goldenberg-Hart for her help in assembling this, and to Michael Buckland and Joan Lippincott for some very helpful suggestions.

between sites to build a correlated, multi-site, view of who you are, what you are doing, and what your interests are.

There are also offerings that straddle consumer and business markets, or focus on businesses; notable pioneers here are Google (with Docs, Calendar and other services), Microsoft, to some extent Yahoo, and a few other players.

When we look at applications in the cloud, the technical definitions go out the window. Really we face a set of technologies and business models coming together to advance a world view that most of what you are doing in your interactions with information of various kinds (and with other people) has come off of your desktop, it has come off of machines you control and actually the locus of control over your destiny has moved out of your hands. Someone else holds and controls the tools and sometimes the content as well, and sometimes the content is not very useful without the tools to display and manipulate it.

You may have seen, earlier this year, the offering of Office 365 from Microsoft, which basically moves away from a desktop centric application suite to a very attractively priced network provision of these application services. Google, in a very real sense, was already there with a range of services like Google Docs. But while the Google applications suite was *created* as a cloud-based set of services, Microsoft is following a deliberate product development strategy in that they are moving away from, or at least starting to move away from, a very profitable franchise that is built on local software into something that is cloud-based.

Most recently and really the most aggressively framed development in this area that I have seen at scale is what Adobe has done, where basically they have said they are not going to *sell* you software anymore (well, more correctly, license you a local copy of software); those days are over, your only option is to rent it through the cloud.

Now contrast that to Microsoft's position, which I interpret as: we will be happy to take your money if you want to license ("buy") it locally, or we will give you a financially attractive deal at least for the moment if you want to rent it through the cloud because we are trying to drive business that way – but we will accommodate users and take their money either way. Adobe took a very, very aggressive stance and basically said we are moving to this new environment. Period. A little later in this talk we will return to these developments: I will argue that software as a service has some really scary implications when we consider interactions with the creation, the character, the management and the access to the broad cultural record.

Enough about clouds in general.

I am going to cover two sets of issues tonight: one is around the character of the cultural record itself and how some of these developments in cloud computing are changing the nature of the cultural record – with particular emphasis, frankly, on the sort of personal or individual realm as opposed to the large-scale commercial realm. The other thing I am going to talk about is how the ways in which we manage and provide access to the cultural record, both the record we have already accumulated over centuries and centuries of human activities, and the record going forward, how the way we manage and offer access to that record changes because of the cloud. I think we will see some very interesting things quickly in the access arena, and I will start there.

I want to stress that even when we are talking about technical clouds, there are a number of these, and do not make the mistake of thinking they play particularly nicely with each other: they are all a bit different. It is quite a pain, in many cases, quite a substantial and expensive and time-consuming technical enterprise to migrate something from one cloud to another.

Furthermore, particularly when you think about data-intensive applications, as many of us in the world of scientific or scholarly data curation, libraries, management of cultural materials think about, when you think about those sorts of things, bandwidth is a big issue. If it takes you months to get your data in and further months to get it out because you are constrained by some limited bandwidth bottleneck at the entry point to the cloud or you discover that the cost of bandwidth in and out of a given cloud is very expensive (and hence the switching costs to move from one cloud to another are very high), or if you face these problems because you want to use data stored across multiple clouds, you suddenly realize that this world of computational utilities that we have been dreaming about since the 1960s and now, in some ways, can see manifest in the clouds, is still a place with lots of barriers and bottlenecks and many of them revolve around the availability of bandwidth; you need to look very carefully at how things are interconnected and where your data flows to and from.

So, for instance, you see commercial players like Amazon or Microsoft offering compute-on-demand services; you might think these would be of great interest to people who needed extra peak load cycles for some reason, who are doing high-end scientific computing. They are indeed of some interest, but until fairly recently there were real barriers. You did not have the direct connections and peering between the research and education networks (where most of the data was housed) and these commercial clouds. A lot of research computing (particularly with irregular demands for cycles, that might be driven by observational campaigns or natural events that occur irregularly) turns out to also be data intensive as well; it is not like a transaction peak over a common (fairly small) commercial database already in the cloud that takes place for Internet florists on Mother's Day. The problem has been getting data to where the cycles are.

Another likely bottleneck (and we'll come back to this a little later as well) is the mismatch between the bandwidth available to an individual – what you can get at home from DSL, from cable broadband, or from fiber (if you are lucky enough to have it) at some reasonable price – the mismatch between the kind of data rates you can get there and the kind of bandwidth provisioning available to support activities that take place *inside* a Cloud. One implication of this mismatch means that you cannot casually say "I'm going to do a really big data extract and move it down to my desktop and deal with it." You cannot do that: not because your desktop machine is not big enough or because you do not have enough local disk storage, but because in many countries the policies that surround the deployment of consumer broadband have left us in situations where that broadband is really not very broad, and it is probably not going to get a lot better real soon, as is unquestionably the case in much of the United States right now. While there are some wild cards in the States like Google's threat (or promise) to go out and connect every home in a couple of select cities with direct fiber and really fast, inexpensive connections, it looks pretty grim for the next few years for most people.

3   Access to Content: Open Data and Computational Capacity

Now let me talk a bit about how Clouds change the management and access of the cultural record and then we will move on to what they are doing to the record itself for the remainder of our time.

Access to digital information has always implicitly required and assumed that a certain amount of computational power is being made available for search, navigation and display of content. Historically when we thought about doing things like reading journal articles online, reading a newspaper online, reading a book online, these access activities took place at human speed, at the speed of eyes, at the speed of the human reader flipping virtual pages; the cost of the actual amount of computation you had to provide to support these activities per user was (at least in recent years) relatively small and steadily diminishing over time as we happily rode the curve of Moore's Law, computing getting cheaper every year. (There was also some cost for searching, for discovery and navigation, but that was also computationally reasonable, at least for the constrained search and navigation options offered by typical sites oriented towards reading or viewing.) The notion of being able to bring up Web-based services that would support vast numbers of concurrent readers was pretty manageable economically. Yes, there was cost associated with it, there was engineering associated with it, but this sort of cost per eyeball was a tractable kind of thing you could write off through advertising revenues if you were a commercial entity, you could write it off within an operating budget if you were a government or not-for-profit entity. (To be sure, streamed media – audio or video – is substantially more challenging and more costly, though clearly not out of reach, based on the amount of this material available on the network either free or through advertising support.)

I think you are seeing around the world (certainly in the United States) a substantial amount of policy emphasis on opening up access to government information, whether it's textual, numeric, or imagery, or whatever, and also opening up access to both writings and underlying data that are the result of government-funded research. These developments are a key part of the whole open access movement, and indeed even broader trends towards openness in scholarship. A lot of the focus inside academia in the last few years has been around scholarly articles and what this means for journal publishing, and around, particularly in recent years, the sharing of underlying research data as well, when these are the result of federally-funded research. And there are additional, compelling, arguments advanced in various contexts that argue for open access to scholarly publications and scholarly data independent of funding source. In May 2013 in the United States you saw an executive order from the President – which doesn't seem to have gotten nearly as much press as the discussion of open access for research – basically telling all of the executive branch agencies in the United States that they should be planning, going forward, for making all of their data publicly available, unless there was some good reason not to (confidentiality and privacy, security, something like that) but the default action would be they should be designing systems that open these data assets up to the public. There are also very broad movements urging cultural memory organizations worldwide to open up digital representations of their holdings (unless prohibited by copyright or other barriers) for public access as well.

What it means to make these materials "open" is a very critical question. Now, what is starting to happen is that we are starting to see these traditional human readers who flip virtual pages or study drawings on screen and are not very computationally intensive getting joined by a menagerie of computer programs that want to do text mining and data mining and image recognition and cross comparison and indexing and all kinds of fascinating stuff, some of which is relatively well understood and some of which is rapidly evolving, experimental, cutting edge research technology. These software instruments are showing up and wanting access to large collections of data and they are joining human readers in looking through large collections of text, images, video and other material designed for more direct human apprehension. So all of a sudden, we are starting to see these ideas about open access taking on this problematic dimension of computational provisioning. As a content provider it's no longer enough to say I need enough disk space to house the data I am obligated to provide access to, and then I need some relatively light accompanying computing capability to let human beings look at it. Now all of a sudden to really deliver meaningful, comprehensive open access, you need to be able to provision a lot of computational capacity, and in many cases come up with methods for rationing its use, as the demand seems open-ended.

Many areas – certainly many scholarly disciplines or sub-disciplines – are just getting too big and growing too fast for humans to cope; we now see measures of disciplinary literature growth that are counted in *articles per minute*. Nobody is going to keep up with the literature of a sub-discipline that's growing at a rate of an article every 10 minutes, even. Or, I would invite you to consider the mismatch between upload and view rates on something like YouTube; they upload something like *a hundred hours viewing time* worth of video every minute of every day, or something in that area. These are numbers that basically say that without a lot of computational capacity, you really cannot cope effectively with existing knowledge bases or content collections, you cannot analyze developments or allocate your limited reading time well.

Consider the problem of the historian of the 21st century: say they're trying to write a history of one of our recent presidents in the United States. The issue there is not if they can get access to the material; the issue there is that there is more material there than they can read in five lifetimes and somehow they need a lot of computational help to classify it and to identify the relevant parts. Imagine the special collections of the 21st century that are being accessioned in libraries right now: in the past, a library or archive might get a few dozen cartons of somebody's papers and correspondence. Today that personal collection might involve thirty-five years of collected email, hundreds of thousands of messages, and a pile of disk drives full of documents. The issue there again is going to be there is no way human beings are going to dig through all of that; in the future it is going to be historians and biographers and political scientists and other scholars partnered with computational tools that need to interact with these special collections.

I would just note parenthetically that there are also tough problems on the curatorial side of many archives and special collections here; one of the big ones is redaction. When the size of the print record was pretty small, you could find enough human beings to go through and redact indiscreet things and pull items that should stay private; in government settings you could make decisions about whether something was classified and whether it could be declassified. Now you have just an unmanageable problem when you start talking about things like government records or personal papers. Can you let users compute on them and then select a few things that a human curator might go through and appraise and redact if necessary? Can you let that computation happen safely without too much implicit information leaking out to cause trouble? These are strange and wonderful new areas of research that are taking the stage as we struggle with this environment.

Finally, I want to really stress that the need for computational capability is not just to permit humans to do the kind of access or research that they have traditionally done in an environment where the amount of content available has grown unmanageable. It is also central to being able to ask very new kinds of questions, whether about graphs of social, intellectual, economic or other connectivity; about the outcomes of inference or the identification of consensus or contradictions within very large collections of text or data; about statistical correlations and the identification of outliers. One could, for example, attempt to run an analysis of major collections of Greek antiquities worldwide to computationally attempt to characterize an "archetypal" version of a common kind of vase, and to characterize the patterns of variation, and then link this to the geography of excavation sites.

So let us return to this issue of access implying computation and connect it to clouds. We are now moving into an environment where more and more kinds of access actually require meaningful amounts of computation and we have some hard questions here. One is *where* does the computation happen; the way we answer this largely determines who chooses and provides the tools, and who sets the limits on what you as a user of information can do. Let us look very quickly at a few scenarios.

Let us imagine that I want to do a complex computation over a substantial slice of the recent literature in molecular biology – perhaps, say, 750,000 articles. Or a big slice of the Twitter archive. If the publishers or other repositories housing them will let me download them (not at all clear, in part because some publishers do not agree that this kind of download and compute scenario is part of open access, or something that they need to support in offering public access, on a policy basis; in part because you may not have the storage needed to hold all these articles, or the bandwidth to your local resources that will allow you to download them in reasonable time and at reasonable cost; in part because some repositories may not have the computational provisioning even to support this kind of bulk downloading, or may rate limit it to reduce the computational impact, though this translates into a very long download time); given all these caveats, I could download them and do my computations locally.

Or, in theory I could send my computation over to the repository. Well, how many sites do you know who say "send me your arbitrary programs, I'm happy to run them and see what they do on my site, what fun"? No, what they will do is they will sandbox you into some kind of virtual machine environment that is very carefully constrained and isolated – but this is hard to do, and a big security risk, and they do not have the computational capacity anyway, so running your "programs" on the repository site is unlikely in many cases. Or they will support a small, constrained set of high-level queries where they can bound the computational demand and the functionality of the queries.

(I will note in passing another issue. Literatures are, and will be, most typically scattered across large numbers of repositories or libraries. So from the user perspective, it is not working with one source of content, but many in parallel. This also changes the tradeoffs and indeed even the feasibility of shipping queries to the data rather than copying the aggregated data somewhere and computing on it.)

There is a debate that is simmering which comes down to this: are open-access articles going to be liquid, mobile, or are we going to, for most practical purposes, have the tools of text mining defined by the publishing community because you will need to run those tools in their environment? Will publishers only let you run specific tools or will they charge you extra if you want to run other tools that are computationally intensive; they may choose to let you only run things that are fairly inexpensive. You can ask the same question not just about publishers (and other repositories) with regard to articles but also more generally about cultural memory organizations and the materials that they house. The Library of Congress got some publicity about a year and a half ago, when it was announced that they were going to preserve and host the Twitter archive. So they have now got these data feeds coming in from Twitter. Housing them on disk is not only a moderate problem; if you talk to the people there the really intractable problem is how they provide meaningful access to this resource because of the scale of computational provisioning necessary. It is a question of where does the Library of Congress get computational capacity to deal with the kind of queries that people are going to want to run across this database, which are not simply "show me tweet 21,000,000,992"; they are going to be asking questions about the nature of the social graph, retweet patterns, and things that are genuinely expensive to compute.

So back to the clouds. Can we do some of this computation in the clouds, where at least in some cases there is already a public market in computational resources and an infrastructure (albeit a heavy-handed one) for isolating users? Can we imagine an environment where if you really want to dig into the treasures of a poorly funded cultural heritage organization or maybe not even poorly funded, but just one without infinite resources, the deal is you *buy* some computing cycles in a part of the same cloud that the cultural heritage storage organization occupies so that the data transfer is manageable within that cloud, (you certainly in most cases if it is a big collection of data, cannot download it yourself because the consumer broadband infrastructure is incapable of handling this, or prices it out of reach).

There are some other interesting variations one can imagine here. In some parts of the United States now (and I think other countries as well), we are asking questions about the role of libraries and particularly public libraries in society going forward. We are also asking questions about how much bandwidth should a public library have and what would they do with it. There are at least a few experiments that are starting to install gigabit and upward connectivity into public libraries. One can imagine public libraries serving as a safety net for a failed consumer broadband policy, at least in some locales, and at the same time also providing some help to people who need assistance in doing this kind of analysis of cultural memory content, a very interesting and unexpected set of developments.

Another angle is this question about the mobility of computation, the idea of sending your queries or computations to the data rather than pulling the data to where you have got computational capacity and control. This is an issue that has a very, very rich history; it has a history that reaches into the construction of query languages, into distributed computing, into the design of distributed computing protocols, the allocation of function between client and server, virtualization and virtual machines. If you look at the ideas that motivated the development of things like Java, there again this notion of protected computing environments, where one could safely deliver computation to a data environment, go back all the way to the mid-1980s, when Bob Kahn and Vint Cerf (names you will recognize from the foundational developments of the Internet), actually developed a vision of what they called *knowbots*, which were a way of specifying and packaging computation and moving it to data. (The key citation here is *The Digital Library Project Volume I: The World of Knowbots, 1988;* it is online.) All of these things now are resurfacing in very interesting new ways in the worlds of big data and cloud environments.

Clearly there are lots and lots of details here, the details are really interesting, and they are really complicated and really situational. One of the great challenges I think is going to be coming up with better tools to make more and more of the user community able to do computational things with literature and data and we are seeing a huge amount of work in that area right now. Look at the impact of something as simple as the Google Books Ngram Viewer, where you now have a whole line of research that basically says "I'd like to look at a century and a half of text starting in 1750 and look at how the usage of certain phrases came and went across that century and a half and in what kind of books and in what kind of context." A lot of the developments in digital humanities are in part efforts to get better tools interacting with very large data collections and get such tools to the stage where humanists do not have to also be computer scientists but can just collaborate with them. This is abstraction as an enabler, a democratizer, rather than as a means of restricting functionality. I suspect that the HathiTrust Research Center will be a very important nexus in developments here.

I will give you one other example, which I think really illustrates how much progress has been made. Cast your mind back if you have been around that long, to let's say 1990 and to the wonderful emerging world in the early 1990s of so-called GIS Geographical Information Systems. You will remember some very expensive proprietary tools, you will remember that many research libraries had this one specialized person, the GIS librarian who worked with these geospatial data sets and these very complicated tools and would work one-on-one with PhD students who needed to weave them into the work they were doing. Compare that to Google Maps, Google Earth and similar products from other competitors. We have forgotten how quickly we progressed from a time when geospatial data was a very specialized preserve of a few people and now, when basic functions are accessible to a very significant amount of the interested people out in the world.

4   The Changing Nature of the Cultural Record Itself

This is all that I have time to talk about with regard to clouds and access to the cultural record. Let us turn, in our last 20 minutes or so, to the related but quite distinct question of what is happening to the *nature* of the cultural record.

Let us simply stipulate that the cultural record is a very big and diverse and messy thing. We could spend a lot of time that we do not have tonight, delineating its boundaries and looking at where new growth is taking place. I am not going to talk too much about — in fact hardly at all — the sort of commercial side of this, about how we save books and movies and sound recordings and photographs and images that find their way into the consumer marketplace and the various instrumentalities that we have around that consumer marketplace to ensure that those things get saved. There are a lot of the complex and important issues that are showing up there as well but instead I want to focus on the individual, the consumer if you will, and to recognize that a great deal of the cultural history that we have out there really is not published (or was not originally intended to be published), it really was not developed for money, it was done by some individual because they were sharing their thoughts, ideas, knowledge with someone else, they were writing letters, they were capturing their experiences, they were making art, not necessarily for the purposes of commerce but just for the love of the making of art, all kinds of motivations and that has come down to us in our archives, in our library collections especially our special collections, in other cultural memory organizations.

If you look at great research libraries you know much of the core uniqueness and distinctiveness of their individual collections are in their holdings of personal, and in some cases institutional, materials that were never published; that is what makes them such rich resources for research. What happens when personal lives get scattered across the clouds? I would suggest that already we are seeing most people moving very quickly away from an era of "having their stuff physically" – first in filing cabinets and cartons and shoe boxes and albums full of photos, and home movies, and sound recordings and more recently on various kinds of portable storage media and hard drives. Today, more and more their stuff is scattered around the net, around the clouds, much of it is in the custody of commercial services where you may or may not be able to get it out, where the commercial services may or may not give you a lot of notice if they decide to go out of business or simply become bored with managing your stuff, where heirs may not even be able to find it in the first place. We have interesting examples of all of those kinds of phenomena happening.

What we really see taking place here, I would say, is something that is beyond technical; it is really a whole restructuring of the relationship between human beings and the things they create and record and share, where a lot more of that has been pushed out into hard to define kinds of places on the network, where the obligations for stewardship are unclear at best, sometimes actively off the table. And it is not just things that people are putting on social media: it is calendars and mail and all kinds of fragments of daily life — those have all moved away, they have moved out there. The term "digital lives" has come into popular use to describe these aggregates of material. If you really want to intuitively capture this as specifically as possible and understand how deep the shift is, think of the notion of personal effects: used to be somebody died and somebody, some member of their family or the executor of their will or someone, would come and sort out their personal effects. These personal effects were mostly physical things, some of them were bought things, they might be books, many of them might be family photos, they might be letters, or the electric bills that strange people you know file for 35 years, month after month, just because they get them and they file them... but there was this sort of notion of personal effects that were physical, that you could find and sort and transfer possession of.

Today when people die, we move into this enormous ambiguous terrain, a legally gray area, a gray area in practice and procedure and custom, where simply getting an inventory is almost impossible, you know. Do you know all the accounts that people you are close to have on all of those systems out there? Do you know their passwords? Do you know what the policies of those various organizations are in terms of you show up and say I am the heir of so and so and I would like access to their account? Do you understand the potential consequences of impersonating the deceased because you have their logon information? Do you know what is likely to vanish in thirty or sixty days because nobody is paying the bill to the storage cloud or application service that is hosting it? There have been some really heartbreaking cases here where, for example, young kids go off to war, they do not come back and their parents want to ensure that their Facebook page or MySpace site, or whatever, is saved, and sorting out the right arrangements and access has proved to be very complicated or failed totally. This is an area also where there is tremendous variability from nation to nation; the law on this is anything but settled but that just illustrates the level of fragility we have come to regarding personal digital materials and the extent to which all of the personal information that people have has migrated out into these various clouds that are now an integral part of the fabric of our cultural record, for better or for worse.

5   A Few Comments: Software as a Cloud Generated Service

I want to close by spending a couple of minutes on a few comments about the recent move of software to the cloud, the examples from Microsoft, Adobe, Google and others that I mentioned earlier, and even the idea that you are starting to see now of applications that are self-updating all the time (in various architectural distributions between cloud and desktop). If you really step back and look at many of the issues around the meaningful longevity of digital information and our ability to manage this longevity (by which I mean more than preservation, I mean the ability to be able to continually, reliably use the digital information in mainstream ways, without heroic measures, antique hardware, and the like – it is the difference between obsolescent and major archival challenges, perhaps), one of the things that is at the heart of our ability to handle this is being able to connect and pace software revisions to the management of data. Particularly in a world where we sometimes find software vendors that behave irresponsibly, disingenuously, and destructively with regard to back compatibility; the history here is not good and does not fill one with confidence. Also remember that given the interdependence and layering in software environments a decision by one vendor (especially at the operating system level) may mean that a great deal of software from other vendors stops working suddenly.

Standards are a certain amount of protection against surprise or forced obsolescence because, at least on a good day, sometimes you can get software vendors to adhere to standards and give you some advance warning when they are going to stop supporting them; you often have a broader choice of tools and marketplace alternatives if it is a well-established market standard. But standards are sometimes there when you want them, sometimes they are not; sometimes the adoption rates are high, other times in other areas the adoption rates are smaller.

So this sets up a very, very dangerous situation: imagine a couple of years from now that we are operating in a cloud software environment. I do not own any software anymore; indeed, what I am doing is paying a subscription for it. And when I sign on to use the service, I get whatever the vendor decides is the current version.

Now there are a couple of bad things that happen here. One, of course, is that if I hit some financial reversals: I cannot use my content anymore because I can no longer afford to pay the rent on the tool to use it, or perhaps I have chosen (or been forced) to store my content in the application-as-a-service environment, and I have lost my content too. Worse: you connect up and your updates start applying and when all your updates are finished, you discover that the latest and greatest version of whatever this is does not support some of your old formats and now all of a sudden, you have a collection of orphaned content. Maybe the vendor did not think this was important; maybe you missed the announcement; maybe you were away for a while and did not realize that you had a one-month window to convert from old to new format in preparation for the new release. But the net effect is the same.

In that situation, you cannot do any of the things that we do today when that happens because of a new software release, you cannot say "well I think maybe I'm not going to go with that update and I'll go to my backup and I'll run last year's version for a couple of years while I figure out what to do with all the material that would otherwise be orphaned". You cannot go on E-bay looking for an old version of the software to run on a new machine because the old version of the software disappeared into the vaults of the software cloud provider and is never going to be seen again – withdrawn from marketing really means gone! Basically what the applications clouds do is raise the specter of having the pacing of the ability to read old formats move entirely to the mercy of the software suppliers.

I think that how we operate in this world is an enormous challenge; it has a little bit of an echo of some of the stories that have been going around recently about electronic book readers going wild and deciding that you are in a country where this material is not licensed so it is just going to erase your library. Or, of course, the classic but true story from a few years ago of Amazon erroneously deciding that the version of Orwell's 1984 that they had been making available was in fact covered by copyright and needed to be disappeared from all the Kindles in the field. That actually did happen (and of course the fact they picked that book is just mindboggling but this is actually a true story). We really begin to see here, I think, the potential that not just content but software becomes much more deeply implicated in this cloud setting of some very problematic unintended consequences for our ability as individuals to preserve material and consequently for that material to find its way into the more formal and more protected cultural record across time.

6   In Conclusion

Our time has run out. So, I hope I have given you a couple of broad ideas to consider.

One is the increasingly deep involvement of computation in access to content. I think there is no question that we are moving into a political environment and into a set of scholarly norms that place a great deal more emphasis on open and public access to data, access to writing, access to primary source material that is in various hands. That access increasingly includes computation and we do not have good strategies yet for how we are going to provision and fund the necessary computational resources, how we are going to manage the relationships between computation and content, and where we are going to situate that computation between the stewards of content and the people who need to use that content. Similarly, I hope I have given you some things to think about in terms of the new relationship between the individual's accumulation of memories and observations and creative works and records, and the world of commercial services and social media that are spread across the cloud, and some of what that may mean for the future of the cultural record and our ability to preserve this record.

I also hope I have given you some questions to ponder about as you grapple with the rapidly-developing idea of software as a service that is cloud-based, and that, as a consequence of that move to the cloud, really starts to take individuals out of the control of the character and rate of evolution of that software in a much more aggressive and comprehensive way than has been the case in the past. I am not at all certain that we collectively understand the implications of this, particularly as it relates to the preservation of "digital lives" at the personal level, which, in turn, also has implications for the future of the overall cultural record. I cannot urge you enough to think very carefully and critically about this, because the stakes are very high.

Thank you.

Cloud Computing Beyond the Obvious:
An Approach for Innovation

Christian Verstraete

Chief Technologist, Cloud Strategy Team at Hewlett-Packard Company,
Hermeslaan 1A B-1831 Diegem, Belgium
christian.verstraete@hp.com

Abstract. In an ever more digital world, cloud computing has emerged as a new way of doing things for IT. But is it just that or is it a fundamental transformation of the role of IT in business? Isn't IT slowly becoming the way business is done? In this talk, I will discuss how the combination of cloud computing, mobility, social media and big data is fundamentally transforming our lives and our way of doing business. Beyond just doing IT differently, it opens up new opportunities for business people and opens up brand new avenues of innovation. Using real examples, I will illustrate the tremendous opportunities technology provides today and in the near future.

Keywords: Cloud computing, innovation, social media, the Internet of Things, big data.

1   Introduction

I am really glad to be in Limerick.[1] What I want to talk to you about is how cloud computing can really help us and how it will really change the way we are doing things, how life is going to be different and what we are actually going to do.

2   Cloud Computing

Let me describe how cloud computing gives us immense opportunities to really be able to do new things and to do existing things differently. Let me give you a simple example. What would you think about walking on the streets in whatever town around the globe and suddenly having an ambulance coming near you, with a guy in a white coat coming down saying "Dear Mr. XYZ could you please come and join us in the ambulance because we spotted that in a quarter of an hour you are going to have a heart attack and we want to avoid that." What do you think? You are going to say,

---

[1] Note: This is a moderately edited transcript of a keynote address given at the 4th International Symposium on Information Management in a Changing World (IMCW), Limerick, Republic of Ireland on September 4, 2013; it clarifies a few additional points, but retains the character of a talk rather than a formal paper.

J.N. Gathegi et al. (Eds.): IMCW 2013, CCIS 423, pp. 14–24, 2014.
© Springer-Verlag Berlin Heidelberg 2014

"hey, I'm young, I exercise, I don't care about that. I'm not subject to a heart attack." OK, but it is one of the possibilities that new technologies offer us.

I have been in the IT industry for a little while. I did my first thesis with punched cards on an IBM mainframe. That dates me. My second one was on a Xerox minicomputer with punched tape instead of punched cards, it was still holes in carton and paper. Today, like all of us, I carry a smart phone with me and I am expected to answer within the next five minutes whatever message I get. The world has evolved. It has evolved due to a set of technology waves. We went through the mainframe wave. The next one was something that people called client-server. We have known the internet, web 2.0; now people argue about web 3.0, 4.0, 5.0. Whatever the numbers is, I do not think that is important. What is really key is this combination of things that we are doing at the moment. I mean here the combination of mobile, social, big data, and clouds. Aberdeen Group calls it SoMoClo. I do not know whether you like that name, I hate it, quite frankly, because I do not think it is obvious what it means. First of all, it is unpronounceable and secondly I do not think it means anything but that there is something out there that is actually allowing us to take advantage of new things. Now, all the elements that are here are not equivalent. Social and big data are really about information and the capability of using and exploiting information. Mobile is about how that information reaches you, the consumer of the information, and cloud is really around the environment that makes it all happen. If you start pulling the pieces together, you really are able to do new things, you can start building new customer relationships, you can start setting up new business models, you can do new products and service combinations, you can get new market approaches and so on and so on.

Now I do not want to tell you just the theory. Let me give you a lot of examples. But, before doing that, what is changing? Well, until now as an individual, as an enterprise, to be able to explore IT in one way, form or fashion, you needed a "data center". It could be as small as a couple of PCs or a couple of servers in a cupboard or could be as large as a couple of football fields. Part of your organization was focused on running all that infrastructure. That is now moving away, that is moving away because there is this feeling that somewhere in the universe there is this unlimited capacity of infrastructure I can tap into. Now, we all know it is not unlimited because everything is limited in the world but it is limited to such a minimal extent that it sounds like unlimited to us, that is one piece.

And then the other piece of the equation that is sort of creeping into everything we do is this whole concept of pay per use. Pay per use is not specific to IT. Today in Brussels, and I am pretty sure in many other countries, if I wish, I can take a bike or a car in a pay per use model. I was talking to an airplane engine maker, and what I did not realize is today most airlines do not buy engines anymore, they pay per use, did you know that? Very interesting. So, that concept is not just specific to IT but it is also used in IT.

3   Time Dimension, Globalization and Innovation

Time is also shrinking. When I joined HP we had a wonderful system that allowed us to get the response from our West Coast business units in three working days. Over the break, I can explain it to you how it worked. It was unmatched and our customers were absolutely flabbergasted. Today, if my respondent has not responded in 10 minutes, I am getting nervous. Time is shrinking. So, we are expected to be on the ball much faster.

The world is at the same time becoming more global and more complex so we need to be able to receive, digest, sequence an ever larger amount of information before we can take a decision. You have to provide feedback faster and faster. That is where that combination of mobile, clouds, big data and social is really going to help us. What are enterprises looking for today? We have gone over the last 10 years and for the ones amongst you who are in the business world, you probably realize that we have gone through an ever increasing cost reductions scheme, and we reduced cost in many companies to the barebones. Now we need to get to something else and people are back into the mood of more innovation, but to be able to innovate, they want the enterprise to be more agile. They want their enterprise to be more responsive, to react faster to opportunities in new geographies, new areas where they can do business, or something else; but the CFOs are out there to make absolutely sure that this happens without extra costs. Now, to be able to do that, what they really need is understanding their markets, understanding their customers much better. At the same time, all our end-users who until 10 years ago were completely IT illiterate, now they facebook and they tweet and they blog and they do all of those things. They are expecting and they are getting a heck of a lot of things free, at the top of their fingertips. Why can't they get the same from their IT department? So what they want is to be always connected, they want to have the information at their fingertips, they want to increase the IT flexibility, so they can get what they want, when they want it, and obviously all of that needs to happen at a reduced cost.

That leads to innovation. Now, innovation is a really interesting topic. The real question, however, is where can I innovate? I believe that there are four key places where you can really start innovation if you are in an enterprise. You can innovate in your business, build new business models, improve existing ones, and create efficiencies working at the business or the process level. I will give you some examples of people who have done that. You could work more and more at the combination of products and services. Think about the arrival of smart TVs. Yesterday, Samsung announced a "Smart Watch". I have no clue what purpose it serves but they announced it. Now you are going to be able to respond to your email by talking to your watch rather than picking up your mobile phone, so you will do it in three and a half seconds rather than five. Fine, okay, I can get that, but what is the added value? I am not sure, but that is a different debate altogether.

These are new combinations. Enterprises move away from just working within the boundaries of their companies and start looking at the whole ecosystem. If you are in the manufacturing industry, you start dealing with your supply chain partners to really create an integrated supply chain that has a much better understanding and can manage things more effectively. You may want to interact with your customers on a much more consistent basis, and, last but not least, you may want to change from an IT perspective. We spend a lot of time in focusing on what Jeffrey Moore calls the systems of records, the basic systems you need to run your enterprise. Today is the time for the system of engagements, the systems that allow you to operate, to collaborate, to be able to do things faster and better as a group of people that want to work together.

Those four classes of innovation are fuelled by technology innovation. I am not an advocate of using technology for the sake of using technology. Technology is there to help you achieve your business better, to help you create those new products, to integrate services, to run your ecosystem better. And clouds, mobility, social and big data are really technologies that will help us moving forward.

4   Social Media

So, enough about theory. Let me give you some examples. And let me start with a really interesting one. About two and a half years ago, Fiat Brazil was asked to create a new concept car, a concept car for an emerging market. I had the chance to talk to the guy who actually set up the whole thing. He said that before they started they expected that the Brazilians would want a large, you know, big car. But they decided that rather than just doing what they thought the Brazilians wanted, they would ask them. So they set up an IT portal. They did something which is called crowd-sourcing, they asked people to help, to critique, to give ideas on that concept car and they ended up with more than 17,000 participants on a day to day basis through participating with the designers to create the car.

And what did they come up with? Something that looked like this: a very small, very efficient car that could get through the traffic, the horrendous traffic of Sao Paulo, Rio de Janeiro and a couple of other cities out there. What was unique was the way they interacted with their potential customers. You know, what was the only critique from their potential customers? That the car actually never got built and sold because in the same process, they got ideas from 17,000 people, they also got 17,000 customers. You know, if you have been participating in building a car, hey, you want one, don't you? So they could have taken it one step further, but that was not the objective of the exercise. This project is called the Fiat Mio. There is a lot that has been written about it. It is really interesting to see how technologies and how approaches focused on social media can actually help us achieve new things, do new things.

Let me give you another example that I like even better. A young guy in the U.S. who created a small product to use with the iPhone. He went through the hassle to take the patents, to find somebody to manufacture it and so on. His product became successful and he sold the company off to an investor. He made lots of money and then he turned around and said, now I need to create something else. He started tossing with ideas of what other product he could invent and finally he said no, that's not what I'm going to do. It was very hard to get this product from idea to market. Let me set up a company that will help people getting products from idea to market. So he set up a website. It is called "quirky.com". You can check it. He proposed that anybody who had an idea anywhere around the world can describe it on the website.

The idea remains his, but the description is used by a panel of potential users, which is anybody that wants to participate, and they decide what the best ideas are by voting for them.

Ideas are bubbling up through a process that is called ideation. Every week they take the top idea. They have a couple of designers who work with the guy that came up with the idea and transform the idea into actual products. They file the patents. They are going to find where and who can manufacture it. And finally they sell the product on the internet and through a distribution channel they built up over the years. The inventor of the idea shares the revenue with the company. They have created a company to do business process innovation. They created a new business process taking advantage of new technologies to do something new, interesting isn't it? This is the process that they have actually put in place.

On the website, you can find some of the products. For example, one product which is really simple: it makes a heck of a lot of money and was invented by a guy out of Norway. You know, these power strips that we all have. I am pretty sure you have been in the situation where you plug in a charger and it sits half way above the next plug, so you cannot use the plug. Well, the Norwegian guy said why don't we make one that can just sort of move around, simple isn't it? Well, he brought that idea to the website and the user community found it a great idea. Quirky created it and they both made a ton of money out of it. So, the submitted ideas do not need to be difficult.

Let me end up with the third example. I have a little story around this one. I was one day on a train to Amsterdam, reading some documents on cloud computing. A young guy is sitting near to me and he says, oh sir, are you in cloud computing? I said yes, and he answered me too. So I asked him, what are you doing and he said well I'm working for a GPS company. Hmm, a GPS company – cloud computing, explain this, I don't see the link. He goes on, well, our GPS company is quite successful. OK and that's an issue, success – issue, sorry I don't get it. He explains, well, the problem is as follows, you're driving along the road, in front of you there is a traffic jam. Your GPS gets a signal that there is a traffic jam and calculates an alternate route. The problem is, all of our GPSs use the same algorithm, so they calculate the same alternate route. Everybody takes the alternate route and, because there are many, you get a GPS enabled traffic jam! Frankly, I had never thought about that one. He said, so, now what we're trying to do is to understand where the different GPSs are, suck all of that information back into the cloud and calculate from a cloud perspective according to how many there are and the situation around the traffic jam alternate routes so that different people can take different routes. We then feed that back to the different GPSs. A way to use cloud computing to really start improving the customer experience. Isn't that great? That is an example of a product/service combination to improve customer experience. So next time you take your GPS, you will think about the GPS-enabled traffic jam. I am pretty sure about that one.

5   The Internet of Things

Okay, but these are just simple examples. The world is actually going one step further. You will hear more and more about something which is called the Internet of

Things. Everything that I have talked to you about today, there is always, in one way, form or shape, a human interaction. Our sensors are becoming more and more intelligent. We are getting more and more of them. Here are some of the statistics of what exactly is happening every minute in the world. Frankly, the one statistic that I love most is that apparently every minute in the world we shoot 208,333 Angry Birds! Now, that is not really something that adds a lot of value but we are seeing a tremendous amount of devices that will be able to provide feedback from the information they process. I started by talking about the importance of using that information to be able to make decisions. The Internet of Things is all about that. It is about pervasive connectivity. It is about the use of smart devices and it is about the better usage of the explosion of information that is actually becoming available to us. So, where can that help? Where do we use these devices? I have put a number of examples together. We track wildlife, we try to really understand what is happening with our global warming, we use it for access controls, etc.

I will give you an example in the area of geophysical mapping, infrastructures, traffic control. Do you realize that when a plane flies for a couple of hours, it generates something like 500 gigabytes worth of information that is actually being processed to understand when the plane needs to be maintained, if something could go wrong, and so on? That is just the start, they are examples of where the use of sensors, the acquisition of that real time information really gives us the capability to take decisions, to understand in detail what is actually happening. So let me give you an example, about a year and a half ago I started talking to a company that is doing surveillance cameras, you know them, they are all over the place. What I did not realize is that in this world that is ever more becoming digital, 90% of the surveillance cameras are still analog. Believe me or not, they are analog and they feed into those tapes that are actually keeping the last two, three, four hours' worth of information. And then the information is wiped out, replaced by the new one, not very efficient.

So the idea we came up with was to digitize that information. Then at least we can store it in digital format. And if we digitized that information, would there be a way that we could start analyzing it? It just happens to be that there are a couple of companies around the world that are able to analyze video information for strange things, but it needs to be digital. These companies started doing that for military purposes and now this is becoming more available. I can analyze the information, I can detect something strange is happening and then I have a decision to make, what do I do with it? Do I warn the owner where he is and feed him back what is actually happening so that he can decide whether he wants to intervene, call the police or do nothing?

This is a completely different experience because in a traditional world when something happens, there is a robbery, for example, the only thing you can do is you bring the tape to the police and hope that they can see something, probably eight hours later or whatever. You hope the information has not been wiped out yet. Here you are getting into real time, you are getting close to what is actually happening. You can take the appropriate decisions because you have started combining the different technologies that I have talked about.

You may remember that in the U.S. a couple of bridges collapsed over the last couple of years. A lot of our infrastructure is old. It was built after the Second World War. So we do not really know how well it holds up. Can we equip our infrastructure with sensors that can actually figure out before something happens that things are not what they should be? We all know that events do not happen at once: there are some signals. The problem is, most of the time we do not take care of the signals because we are unaware of them. Sensors allow us to actually understand that, understand the signals and again make the decision that actually needs to be made.

Now, this brings me to another personal example. About three or four years ago, I got in touch, together with some of my colleagues, with Shell because Shell had a problem. The pumps in refineries occasionally failed and it is enough for one pump in a refinery to fail and you stop the whole refinery. And we all know we do not have too much refinery capacity around the globe at the moment. So they were looking at ways to actually predict when a pump was going to give up so they could repair it during a preventive maintenance cycle. Today what they do is, after the pump has been used a given number of years or months, they actually replace it. That is not the most efficient use because some of those pumps still go on for a couple years but you want to know when they are going to give up.

In the hope of solving that, we looked at a little device that we have created: a 3D accelerometer, which is extremely precise, to actually look at the vibrations. We took the whole Shell team to our labs in Palo Alto where the device had been created to actually go and discuss that project. One of the guys that was present was the chief technology officer from the company and as soon as he heard what the device could do, he stopped and he said no, we are not going to use this device to check pumps, we are going to do something completely different.

What have we done? Well, the area he wanted to look at was seismic exploration. Do you know how you find oil in the ground? It is actually pretty primitive in a way. What you do is you put a bunch of sensors around the place, you then come in with a big truck, like the one that is at the top there, you know. The truck for about 15 minutes says "boom, boom, boom, boom, boom, boom, boom," and you listen to the return of those vibrations and depending on those returns and where they are, you can actually understand the structure of the underground. That gives you a vision of whether there is a possibility of oil being there. The problem is that the devices that they use are about as large as an old telephone. They're called optophones, if I remember right. They cost $3000 apiece. So, the maximum they can put in is about 100,000 of them and, by the way, they need to cable them. So think about 100,000 devices over ten square kilometer with cables. Think about the time it takes to set it up, the time it takes to take it down, the weight and so on. And because you can only put 100,000, you have a certain visibility. You only take a signal every 10 meters or something like that. What he wanted to do was use that sensor, embed that sensor in a device, plug it into the ground and put one every meter. So instead of putting 100,000, put a million of them. Now when you put a million, forget about cables, so you need to go wireless. Well if you go wireless what do I do with energy, what do I do with data transmission? So we have together been reinventing a completely new way of doing seismic data capture.

We have done it and we have started seeing the first results. It has taken us about three years to get there. What basically happens is you have these little, little things, you know they are about this size, 1 square centimeter. On top of it you have a solar panel so that you can recreate and add energy to the batteries because they are going to stay in place for about a week. You have a little antenna because we are going to transmit some data. Indeed, to really measure well you need to measure at 500 hertz, every experiment takes about 15 minutes and the device measures 24 bits so do the calculation: you get the total of a couple petabytes worth of data. Now you just do not transfer two petabytes of data over wireless, there is no way you can do it today with current technologies. So you need to transfer sample data, have a first level of visibility and then when you take all the devices back after a week and after you have run 10-20 tests, what you basically do is you put the device in a holder, which will recharge the batteries and at the same time it will suck the data out. Second thing, how do I know which device is where? Well, the advantage this sensor has is that in 24 hours because of its sensitivity, feeling the changes in traction of moon and sun, it can tell you very precisely where it is. It is quite interesting.

6   Big Data

This is an example of how you use some of those technologies to really be able to start doing new things. Now we are in very early days of all of this, but this is where we are going and this is probably where we will be by the year 2020. It is a whole ecosystem that is actually being built up because now I am going to get these zillions of devices all over the place and each and every one of those devices will give their information or their data, I should say.

Now that data may or may not be used as a piece of raw information. In some situations yes, and in other situations you want it to be aggregated with other pieces of information. So, what you start seeing is the data percolating through a network of aggregators to obtain the level of integration you require for the data to deliver you the information you require. This happens through a net of interrelated technologies, interrelated environments, interrelated infrastructures using cloud computing. It basically gets you the ultimate level of information that you actually want. If you look at the weather, you are not interested in just the temperature just now, you are interested in the complete picture, what is the temperature, what is this, what is that. It is a combination of multiple elements and then that combination together creates you a base of what is being called, for lack of a better term, "big data". I can now go and analyze it to give me what I am really looking for. I can eventually combine that with information that comes with the latest feeds from Irish TV or from the BBC or from CNN. I can combine that with information from anywhere to give me the type of information that I may need do my job.

About six months ago, I wrote down this example. Assume I need to go to a customer. I am arriving in the parking lot, my agenda is up to date so the system knows which customer I am actually going to meet. When I get out of my car it flashes me on my screen: "First of all, don't forget the guy you're meeting just had his birthday yesterday. By the way, he also got his third child. He has been tweeting and a couple of his tweets were rather negative about the company I represent for this and this and that reason. By the way, he had placed an order three months ago, this is the status of the order. Oh, they got an IT problem yesterday this is the latest status, it has just been resolved." So, now I come in and say: "Hello sir, how are you doing? By the way, sorry I'm a day late but happy birthday. And how is your youngest child doing? Oh, I heard you were not really happy about what we're doing, tell me what can I do?" Wow! I have changed the complete interaction with my customer. Why? Because I got a little robot that actually gave me all the information I needed to know right at the time I needed it. You remember, anywhere, anyplace, anytime.

But all this will result in exabytes of data. The creation of that amount of data from a trillion sensors will drive the evolution of our structures, of our infrastructures. We are going to need to change a bunch of things. This is good news because again this will allow us to do more things and to do things differently. One of the things we are going to need to change is our vocabulary. We all know about megabytes, we all know about gigabytes, some of us know about terabytes, some may know about petabytes. I do not know whether you know about any of the others, at least if you are going to get one thing from me today, you're going to get the latest terminology. One point, they still have not agreed whether the "gegobyte" is going to be a "gegobyte", a "geopbyte" or a "geobyte", or whatever. They are still debating about that one.

Try to imagine what amount of data this represents. It becomes unimaginable. You do not want to have to sift through every single byte and every single information of this, you want to get the aggregates to make the decisions. So the technologies are there, it is tying them together, it is delivering what you really need to create that digital experience that is actually becoming the Holy Grail.

A couple of months ago I talked to a CIO of a U.K. company that is selling building materials. They are selling toilets, they are selling bathrooms, but they are also selling bricks, mortar, sand, and all of those things. Not the most exciting and the most innovative company, right? Well, they bought a couple of years ago a U.S. online reseller of the same type of things. I did not know that was existing but apparently it is, and they are looking at how to change the experience of the customer because they realize that their customers are increasingly interacting with them through a variety of different means. They may go to their website and start looking at things, they may go to the showroom, they may call up the call center, they may go and visit one of the sites where they actually do the selling. In every one of those interactions, they are going to leave behind a certain imprint. But because of the fact that all of these are very different channels, nobody actually pulls the pieces together. So, is there a way that I can pull all of the different elements together and create what is starting to get known as a jargon in the market, "the digital persona" of somebody and then use that to engage, to give the person precisely what he or she wants?

Now this becomes a very interesting element because there is an aspect of that which is data gathering. There is also an aspect of that which is much more related to the law, to privacy and to a number of other elements. So, how do I balance between these, how do I balance the fact that I want to give people the best experience with making sure that I keep the privacy that all of us are entitled? How do I understand the meaning of things, understand what people mean, what they want to do, where they want go? It is really important because that allows you to attract people and allows you to better engage with people. It is collecting data from all sources, it is analyzing the data, understanding that data. Probably 80%-95% of that data is unstructured, which makes it a little bit more difficult. The point is pulling them together to achieve the environment and the ecosystems that we want. The mechanisms and tools to do that exist today.

Let me finish off my presentation by giving you a little illustrative example: it so happens that I travel quite a lot so this one relates to me, but I am pretty sure it is going to relate to many of you, too. You know, you are sitting in the plane, you are looking at a film. It is one of my friends who originally created this example and he decided that it was going to be a film from Marcel Pagnol, but that does not matter. And then you get this moment. You are three quarters down the film, you are really into it and then the film freezes and you get this message: "we are 20 minutes before landing and we will shut down the AV system." I want to see the rest of the film. Today, make sure you get back on the same airlines, make sure you do it fast enough so the film is still on the list, remember the moment in the film so that you can fast forward and two or three weeks later you will be able to see the film. What if, let's dream a minute, what if when the plane lands, information is shared, and that information says what I was doing. I reach my hotel, and I enable my hotel to actually take the information about where I was on the film. Information goes back to my hotel and when I reach my room, I have displayed on my TV a message telling me I can finish the film if I want? Hey, why not, a complete digital, a complete different digital experience. Now all the bits and pieces exist today, everything exists; it is just putting them together. So I just try to tease your imagination.

7   Conclusion

I think there are two things that are important in life if you want to really move forward and get along with the way the world is actually changing. First, be curious, do not stop, go and dig into things and understand what happens; you do not need all the details but at least understand what you can get with it. And second, be creative, start pulling unlikely things together. The opportunities are actually endless, you know our biggest limit today is our imagination. We are so much boxed in that we have a tendency to always look inside the box. Every time we come up with an idea we are going to get 27 reasons why this is not going to work. Do not bother about those, okay? There is a whole bunch of new business models that are actually emerging. People are becoming information providers, people are becoming information transformers, information consumers. We are really getting to that information society that we have actually been talking about. The technology is there, most of it is there. It is pulling it together, getting the business model set up, delivering the service, that really needs to be invented.

Remember, everything we do becomes digital. I really got flabbergasted a couple of years ago when talking to a banker, I realized that 97% of money is bits and bytes and computers, there is no physical evidence. When you buy a share, you just get a bit that is changing on the computer of your bank, that is it. Your photos are digital, your films are digital, your books are digital, your conversations are digital... Everything is digital. Technology has been creeping into everything that we actually do. Let us now take advantage of it, let us now explore it. "Imagination is more than knowledge," said Einstein.

And let me finish off with something. You know, when you think about creativity and imagination, the people I like most are the cartoonists because cartoonists have this wonderful capability to pick things together that have no resemblance with each other and express them in one drawing and get a message out. So let me give you one of those examples. You all probably remember that, nearly two years ago, unfortunately, Steve Jobs passed away. Some of you may also remember that a little longer ago, around 1513 BC Moses went to the top of the Sinai and got two stone tablets. What the heck does Moses have to do with Steve Jobs? What do you think? Any idea? Well, at least with one cartoonist they had a lot to do together: "Moses, meet Steve. He's gonna upgrade your tablets..."

That is what I mean. Now, this is done for the purpose of a joke. The same can happen for the purpose of generating a new business, for the purpose of doing something new, for the purpose of helping out humanity, for any other purpose. And I hope that I have sort of shaken your imagination and gotten your cells working a little bit, around how technology in general and the cloud in particular opens up so many new avenues for us to do things that are really exciting. You know what: I am looking forward to the future with a lot of excitement because I think there is a lot of great things that are going to happen and I hope we can all make it better together. Thank you very much.

Cloud Computing: A New Generation of Technology Enables Deeper Collaboration

Marshall Breeding

Independent Consultant, 2512 Essex Place, Nashville, TN 37212, USA
marshall.breeding@librarytechnology.org

Abstract. This keynote address presents a pragmatic approach to cloud computing and its potential to enable libraries to transform their models of resource management, service delivery, and collection discovery.

Keywords: Cloud computing, integrated library systems, library services platforms, library resource discovery services.

1 Introduction

The presentation outlines my view of current trends in the realm of library management systems and the impact that cloud computing has made in that arena. This rapidly-changing domain finds itself in challenging times where library missions evolve in response to changing demands related to collections and patron expectations. Cloud-based technologies and new model automation systems have emerged to help libraries meet these new challenges. This presentation covers these movements along three different tracks: 1) the realm of discovery systems and services that libraries offer to provide access to their resources and their services; 2) resource sharing arrangements that enable libraries access to content beyond their own local collections; and 3) the resource management systems. New developments - many relating to cloud computing technologies- have transpired in each of these areas.

2 Technology Adoption Patterns in Libraries

Libraries have distinctive patterns regarding the implementation of cloud technologies compared to other sectors. As a whole, libraries tend to move to new technologies at a relatively slow pace. Fortunately, a minority of libraries are willing to engage as early adopters willing to test new technologies as they become available. Other presentations in the conference gave a more theoretical view of cloud technologies and information management. Considerable distance, however, lies between the theoretical work that is done in computer engineering and the products and services developed and implemented by libraries to provide access to content and services and to automate operations. This gap between the state of the art and practical products

J.N. Gathegi et al. (Eds.): IMCW 2013, CCIS 423, pp. 25–35, 2014.
© Springer-Verlag Berlin Heidelberg 2014

creates a delay relative to the potential impact that these technologies might have on libraries if they could be delivered more rapidly. Rapid adoption of a technology comes with considerable elements of risk which may not always be tolerable to libraries that prefer to work more within a set of well-proven technologies. Trends relating to the adoption of automation products is documented in the annual "Automation Marketplace" industry report [1].

3   Align Infrastructure with Strategic Mission

To function optimally, libraries must have an automation infrastructure capable of supporting their strategic mission and operational objectives. Technology naturally does not exist as a means in itself, but rather as a set of tools to support the work of a library. Great technology operates relatively transparently, but enables the library to excel in its ability to serve its clients. A mismatch between the critical tasks or activities of the library, what it aspires to accomplish and the capabilities of its automation systems can hinder library success. One of the most glaring issues today relates to library automation systems tightly bound around the model of print borrowing and collections in an era when the electronic and digital collections dominate.

Each sector of libraries sees a different set of trends relative to the shape of their collections and services. Public Libraries, for example, continue to experience vigorous and growing circulation of their print materials. E-book lending has entered as a vital element of service for public libraries, but has not necessarily diminished interest in the print collections and physical spaces. Academic and research libraries, in contrast, generally have experienced more dramatic decreases in the circulation of their print collections as electronic scholarly resources take center stage. Going forward, I hope to see realignment of technology so that it proportionally meets the objectives of libraries relative to print and electronic collections. Over the course of the last two decades, libraries have seen a fundamental shift toward increasingly dominant involvement with electronic materials and it is time for their technology infrastructure to catch up with this reality.

4   Transitioning from Print to Digital

Academic libraries have seen incredible transformation in recent years. In the 1980s, library collections, especially the sciences and technical disciplines, were dominated by print serials, with hundreds of ranges of shelves of bound periodicals which were most actively used. In stark contrast, the print serials collection in recent years sees minimal use since these materials are much more conveniently available through subscriptions to electronic journals and aggregated resources of scholarly content. Many libraries have either discarded or placed the vast majority of their print serials collections in remote storage, making way for collaborative learning spaces or other programs that more directly engage library patrons.

The same kind of shift now is taking place in academic libraries in monographs. Many research libraries continue to have very large legacy print collections. But most academic libraries have reported that they have vastly curtailed current acquisitions of print monographs in favor of e-book collections, often purchased through demand-driven acquisitions.

This transition from print to digital library collections represents a major change, invoking the question of whether the automation systems in place today can continue to optimally handle the new workflows and business processes involved. The overwhelming trend favors ever higher proportions of electronic and digital materials with lower spending on print. That said, library collections will likely not reach a point in the next decade or two where they consist entirely of digital materials. Some amount of print and other physical materials will persist for the long-term future. The proportions will change over time in favor of the digital and the print. The future of library collections will become increasingly multi-faceted and not quickly evolve into purely digital formats.

If that assumption proves true, libraries will increasingly require automation systems designed to handle complex collections comprised of multiple formats, primarily to manage electronic and digital resources but that can also efficiently manage print and physical inventory. The current legacy systems, however, were originally designed during the era when print dominated. These systems that were developed for print, were later updated with an ability to manage electronic resources. In many cases libraries have implemented separate applications or utilities to manage their electronic resources. In this phase when academic libraries spend most of their collection funds on electronic resources, they need the appropriate management and discovery tools.

5   Transitions in Metadata

Much has also changed in the area of metadata used to describe library collections. The MARC formats that have been employed in library automation systems for the last 30 years are poised for change. For the last few years, many libraries have been busy implementing new cataloging rules. RDA, Resource Description and Access, is currently beginning to replace AACR2 as the principle cataloging rules used by many national and academic libraries. This transition has been quite time-consuming and expensive for technical services departments, with only incremental benefits in how these records can be used in management and discovery systems. The implementation of RDA has been especially painful given that many of these technical services departments are already under tremendous pressure to operate more efficiently and with fewer personnel.

The next change in library metadata will be even more drastic. The Initiative for Bibliographic Transformation underway at the Library of Congress has produced a proposed new format that brings bibliographic description of content items into the realm of linked data. This new BIBFRAME structure (see Bibframe.org) represents a mapping of the MARC formats into the RDF triple-stores and the conceptual arena of linked data. The conversations regarding BIBFRAME are still underway and have not been operationalized in any library management system, but warrant close attention given the intense interest in bringing the growing universe of linked data into library information infrastructures.

As libraries become involved with other types of collections, other XML-oriented metadata formats such as Dublin Core, VRA, MODS, METS, and EAD have seen increasing use. These materials are often managed through separate platforms that employ these specialized formats. The vision of many of the new library services platforms includes a more comprehensive approach to managing library resources. To achieve this ambition, these platforms must be able to work with many forms of metadata. The flexibility in metadata management must also include the ability to accommodate new formats that may evolve in future years. Hard-coding any specific metadata format into the systems will ensure that they will eventually become obsolete.

The concept of open linked data stands poised to effect major changes in a future wave of library technologies. The move from AACR2 to RDA has been a very expensive and laborious transition, with a narrower set of tangible benefits in the way that library collections are managed and presented to library users. As changes of greater magnitude loom, I hope that libraries are able to navigate the transition expeditiously and in ways that will achieve more transformational results.

6   Cycles of Technology Culminate in Cloud Computing

Libraries should also be ready from a paradigm shift in the way that they deploy their computing and information infrastructure away from local servers and storage to cloud-based technologies. Cloud computing and applications based on the service-oriented architecture are becoming increasingly adopted in many different kinds of organizations and ICT sectors.

There are many different flavors of cloud computing from which any organization can choose depending on its business needs, security concerns, and policy or legal requirements. Private, public, and local clouds offer different models of resource deployment, data segregation, and hosting locations able to meet these varying requirements [2].

Libraries can achieve many tangible benefits as they move to cloud computing. In contrast to the incumbent model that requires locally installed desktop software, cloud computing generally delivers software through Web-based interfaces and eliminates the need for local servers. Moving to cloud computing enables greatly simplified administration of library automation systems. A library automation system based on client/server architecture, for example, involves an onerous process of installing updates, where new client software may be needed to be deployed on hundreds of workstations. This labor-intensive task consumes considerable time for the library's technical personnel that could otherwise be spent on more worthwhile activities.

The transition to Web-based interface provides many other benefits and flexibility in the way that library personnel and patrons make use of technology-based services. Through concepts such as Responsive Web Design, applications can be easily used across many different types of devices, including smart phones and tablets in addition to full-sized laptop and desktop computers. Given that the adoption of mobile computing continues to rise dramatically, it is essential for libraries to quickly implement interfaces friendly to these devices. Libraries that lack fully mobile enabled interfaces for patron-facing services risk losing an increasing portion of their customers by year. This accelerated trend toward mobile adoption in the consumer sector should prompt libraries to be very aggressive in deploying services that work across all categories of devices. The sluggish way in which libraries have previously moved to new technologies must be accelerated to maintain relevancy and to meet patron expectations through this current phase of change.

The current change resembles previous phases in the history of computing. The earliest phase of library automation took place during the time of mainframe computers. The mainframe-based ILS products relied on very expensive central computers, with character-based interfaces accessed through networks of display terminals with new computational capabilities of their own. These mainframes had very limited capabilities of processing and storage by today's standards, were very expensive, and required highly technical software and hardware engineers to maintain. A new generation computing infrastructure in libraries based on client/server architectures displaced the mainframes beginning in the mid to late 1980s. These client/server systems took advantage of the desktop computers that were beginning to proliferate in libraries in conjunction with more affordable mid-range servers. This generation of library automation systems offered graphical user interfaces for staff and patrons designed to be more intuitive to use than the character-based interfaces of the previous era that operated through cryptic commands or textual menus.

Once the era of client/server computing was in full force, software development had to adjust accordingly. As organizations decommissioned their mainframes, developers began porting or developing software designed for the operating systems, distributed computing models, and graphical environments consistent with the client server architecture.

We see the same kind of fundamental shift in computing architectures playing out in recent years as the era of client/server gives way to cloud computing. In this transition between preferred technology architectures we see two threads among those who develop major library systems. One approach works to reshape existing platforms incrementally toward Web-based interfaces and the service-oriented architecture. This evolutionary method can deliver a more gradual transition toward systems more technically viable by today's standards. They require considerable effort in re-engineering products, but are generally able to reuse some of the code base and preserve functionality that may have matured over time. Alternately, this transition also provides the opportunity to build entirely new products specifically designed to be deployed through modern multi-tenant platforms and with a fresh look at functionality. The evolutionary approach can be seen in integrated library systems that have been substantially reworked to encompass a more inclusive set of resource management capabilities and to gradually implement Web-based interfaces for staff. The new genre of library services platforms includes many examples of the revolutionary development through the creation of entirely new products with an entirely-new codebase written through current programming methods, software architectures, with functionality designed without the baggage of existing systems, and able to be deployed through multi-tenant software-as-a-service.

7   Beware of Marketing Hype

Cloud computing today finds a high level of acceptance in most libraries. In the early phase of this technology cycle many organizations worked on educating libraries regarding the virtues of cloud computing, giving reassurance to its ability to meet the needs of libraries in a reliable and secure way.

As cloud computing has become popular, some organizations have begun to employ the term as they market their products. The term "cloud computing" tends to be applied to scenarios where a vendor hosts the server portion of a client/server application as well as those deployed through true Web-based software-as-a-service. Since "in the cloud" has become more of a marketing term than a technical designation, libraries need to be quite careful with regard to understanding the architecture and deployment options of the systems under consideration. While hosted applications generally represent a positive arrangement for libraries, they also do not necessarily offer transformational potential possible with more full-fledged implementations of multi-tenant software as a service. The term "cloud washing" describes the marketing hype that applies the label of cloud computing without necessarily delivering the technologies consistent with the established architectures.

Even a hosted service that may not meet the modern understanding of software-as-a-service can result in benefits to libraries. The efforts of a library's technical personnel need to be targeted strategically. Taking care of local servers requires considerable time and attention. The layers of security and data protection to responsibly manage local computing and storage infrastructure requires considerable technical expertise and may not play to the core strengths of a library. Large-scale data centers associated with cloud infrastructure providers can employ teams of specialists for each aspect of infrastructure. Relying on externally hosted systems or subscribing to applications through software-as-a-service can free up a library's technical personnel to focus on activities that have a more direct impact on end-user services.

8   Paying for Cloud Computing

Cloud-based services may be priced through a utility model where computing cycles, storage, and bandwidth consumed are metered and charged according to the amount used. Amazon Web Services, for example, employs metered pricing. Customers pay more during peak periods and can scale back to save costs during periods of less intense activity. Utility pricing for cloud-based infrastructure can especially be attractive for software development projects where the use levels remain quite low, and can even remain in the tier of free services. Once the service is ready to be put into production, the resources expected to support higher levels of use are deployed, including redundant components and other configurations needed to provide adequate performance, reliability, and security.

Alternatively some services are priced through fixed monthly or annual subscription fees. This subscription model of pricing prevails in library software, where the company negotiates the amount of the annual fee with the library according to factors such as the components of the system employed, the size of collections, the number of users served, and other factors that represent the scale and complexity of the implementation.

9   Software-as-a-Service

The most common form of cloud computing today involves deploying applications through software-as-a-service. Characteristics of this model include interfaces delivered entirely through a Web browser and with no requirement for local servers. The service will consolidate or segregate uses and data as needed so that individuals or organizations gain access only to their own data, with safeguards in place to prevent unauthorized access. For a mail application such as Gmail, for example, individual accounts can operate both privately and within organizational structures, with the appropriate domain name, user authorizations, branding, and other parameters. Each individual user can see only their own messages, unless explicitly shared within organizational folders. Data architectures have been well established for partitioning multi-tenant software-as-a-service so that each user of a system can access the appropriate data.

Software developers benefit from multi-tenant applications through the ability to deploy a single code base that serves all users of the system with appropriate branding, configuration, and data segregation. New features, security patches, or bug fixes can be deployed once for all users of the system rather than having to install updates on many different server installations and workstation clients.

Many applications deployed through software-as-a- service give users control over the way that new features are deployed. An administrative console gives organizational administrators the ability to manage the configuration and behavior of the system. When new features become available, they may be suppressed initially so that they can be tested and users can be notified or trained as needed before they are activated. Existing features can be improved through incremental changes that do not disrupt the productivity of users as might be the case when major changes happen abruptly.

10   Efficiency and Collaboration

Cloud computing not only enables more efficient and convenient use of applications, but it also brings forward some opportunities that can be transformative to libraries.

While multi-tenant applications must have the ability to limit and segregate access to data, they also come with the ability to share resources very broadly.

While some types of data must be confined within your own organization, there are many areas where information can be shared to the broader community with great mutual benefit. Such multi-tenant, or Web-scale infrastructure, allows libraries to collaboratively build and share critical resources such as bibliographic services, knowledge bases of e-resource coverage and holdings, or centralized article-level discovery indexes.

These highly shared models of automation present many advantages over those based on isolated local implementations of integrated library systems that build individual silos of content. Cloud computing enables workflows that leverage the cumulative efforts of librarians across many different organizations—or even regions of the world—to collaboratively create resources with enormous mutual benefit. These large collaboratively created resources not only allow libraries to operate more efficiently, but this approach also provides ever larger pools of information resources to library patrons and a foundation for resource sharing [3]. Local computing, in contrast, tends to reinforce patterns where each library recreates data transactions redundantly in isolation from their peers.

11   Reshaping Library Organizations and Software Design

This new phase of technology provides the opportunity to develop new library management applications, and to fundamentally re-think their organization and design. The incumbent slate of integrated library systems (ILS) was designed when libraries were involved almost exclusively with print collections.

The classic model of the ILS divides functionality into a standard set of modules including circulation, cataloging, public catalog, serials management, acquisitions, and authority control. Optional modules or add-ons may support reserve reading collections or inter-library loans. Many libraries have structured their organizations in a similar pattern. The transformation of libraries into organizations primarily involved with electronic and digital materials brings the opportunity to reshape both their technical and organizational infrastructure.

In the current model, libraries offer a fairly standard set of services, through desks or offices dedicated to specific activities, most of which are oriented to physical materials. A typical library operates a circulation desk for standard loans and returns of books available in the library, a reserve desk for short-term loans of materials set aside for use in a specific course, inter-library loan to request items not owned by the library. The legacy concepts of circulation, reserves, inter-library loan, branch transfers and related activities may be better conceptualized today as resource fulfillment.

The traditional ILS modules and service points organized around them in the physical library can be reconsidered in favor of alternatives that provide a more flexible service to library patrons. Automation systems likewise can be redesigned to manage and provide access to library resources through workflows optimized for modern multi-faceted collections and not constrained by the increasingly obsolete structure of ILS modules. The transformed nature of multi-faceted library collections that favor electronic materials and new capabilities of resource management systems present an opportunity to reconsider whether the traditional models of service make sense in today's circumstances [4].

12   Open Systems

Libraries today demand more open systems that provide access to data and functionality outside of the user interfaces that come with the system. Libraries today have little tolerance for a closed proprietary system that restricts or completely disables access to its underlying data. Many libraries need to extend the functionality of the system to meet specific local needs. They need to connect systems together to exchange data efficiently. Library automation systems operate within an ecosystem of data that spans many areas of the campus enterprise. The university's student management system definitely manages the accounts of registered students, and this data must be well synchronized with the ILS. The business transactions related to the acquisition of library materials need to be reconciled with the enterprise resource planning or accounting systems of the University. Campus-wide authentication systems should enable all the patron-facing services of the library to operate through a single sign-on mechanism.

In order to meet modern expectations of interoperability and extensibility, library automation systems must be more open than ever before. The primary vehicle for delivering this openness comes through application programming interfaces, or APIs, that allow library programmers to access the data and functionality of the system through a set of well documented requests and responses that can be accessed through scripts of software programs.

In past generations, libraries needing local changes would hope for the ability to customize the internal coding of a system. This model of customization is not sustainable, since the changes made for one organization may not work well for the general release. Also, any local changes would need to be re-implemented with every new release of the software. Local customizations tend to be fragile, with the possibility that any new version of the software may change the underpinnings on which they depend. Rather than expecting to meet local changes by changing the internal coding, modern systems offer a richer set of configuration profiles that meet the needs of most organizations that implement the system and provide APIs to create functionality for local requirements through a more sustainable method.

13   Shared Infrastructure

A modern application, such as a library services platform, provides a base level of functionality through its default user interfaces, but also allows each organization that implements it to create utilities or widgets that extend its capabilities. Many of these local needs may also be useful to other implementers of the system, providing the opportunity for communities of developers surrounding any of these systems to share their code creations and expertise.

Another important consideration relates to how libraries organize themselves relative to their automation environments and the opportunities for large-scale implementations to transform the way they provide access to their collections to patrons. The traditional model of library automation targets providing service to a finite number of facilities organized within a system. A system may be comprised of multiple branches within a municipal library service or a central library and departmental or faculty libraries within a university. Multiple library systems may collaborate to share a library automation system.

The current phase of library automation, with the support of cloud computing technologies, support ever expansive implementations of platforms that enable libraries to automate collaboratively in ever larger numbers. While libraries have shared consortia systems from the earliest phases of automation, their size has been constrained due to the limitations of computing resources. In today's era of cloud computing, the limits of scale seem almost boundless. One of the important trends in recent years includes the consolidation of libraries into shared automation infrastructure, often at the regional, state, or national level [5]. These consolidated implementations allow libraries to automate at a lower cost relative to operating their own local systems and provide their users the benefit of access to massive collections. Some examples of these large shared infrastructure implementations include the State of South Australia where all the public libraries share a single SirsiDynix Symphony system, the country of Chile that provides shared automation based on Ex Libris Aleph coupled with VuFind interface, and the Illinois Heartland Library System based on a Polaris ILS shared by over 450 libraries in the largest consortium in the United States. The country of Denmark has recently launched a project to automate all of the public libraries in the country in a shared system.

Cloud computing stands to support important advancements in library automation, enabling libraries to have a greater impact on the communities they serve. In these times when libraries have fewer resources at their disposal, yet must meet ever increasing expectations to meet the information needs of their clientele, technologies based on cloud computing have considerable potential. A new generation of library services platforms has emerged in recent years that aims to manage resources more comprehensively, to leverage shared knowledge bases and bibliographic services, and to provide open platforms for extensibility and interoperability. Web-scale index-based discovery services provide library users instant access to library collections, spanning all types of resources. This new phase of library automation, built on the foundation of cloud technologies, offers libraries willing to break free from traditional models of automation based on local resources the means to collaborate on a global scale to meet the needs of their communities.

References

1. Breeding, M.: Automation Marketplace: The Rush To Innovate. Lib. J. 137(6) (2013), http://www.thedigitalshift.com/2013/04/ils/automation-marketplace-2013-the-rush-to-innovate/
2. Breeding, M.: Cloud Computing for Libraries. ALA TechSource (2012)

3. Breeding, M.: Next-Gen Library Catalogs. Neal-Schuman Publishers, Inc. (2010)
4. Breeding, M.: The Library Information Landscape Approaching the Year 2050. Information Services and Use 32(3), 105–106 (2012)
5. Breeding, M.: Library Discovery Services: From the Ground to the Cloud. In: Getting Started with Cloud Computing: A LITA Guide. Neal-Schuman (2011)

Evaluation of Conditions Regarding Cloud Computing Applications in Turkey, EU and the USA

Türkay Henkoğlu and Özgür Külcü

Hacettepe University, Department of Information Management,
Beytepe, Ankara, Turkey
{henkoglu,kulcu}@hacettepe.edu.tr

Abstract. Cloud computing services are delivered over the Internet and allow data access from anywhere at any time. In spite of numerous advantages provided by cloud computing, it is important to recognize the potential threats that could include loss of user data. The aim of this study is to raise public awareness on cloud computing by conducting a review of the literature and investigating security and privacy issues related to user data stored on remote servers in the current cloud computing systems. The current laws of United States and all directives and agreements in European Union are examined in order to draw attention to the legal risks and problems in the study. This study shows that there are no legal regulations relating to security and privacy issues of cloud computing in Turkey within the scope of the current cloud computing service agreements.

Keywords: Cloud computing, cloud computing risks, protection of private data, USA data security, EU data security, Turkey data security.

1 Introduction

Although we do not have consensus on a clear definition of cloud computing, it can be defined as a service structure which enables applications to run via a remote server on the Internet environment or as user data stored in a remote server which makes data accessible at any moment. While web interface makes information accessible everywhere and by everyone entitled to access, cloud computing has made information processing usable everywhere and for everyone [1]. However, users are worried about the use of cloud systems, especially where mobile communication and information transfer operations are concerned, because in an informatics era where information is deemed to be of most value, there is a perception that these systems provide inadequate information security. Risks of cloud computing and legal actions in that context have been discussed extensively in the EU and the US [2]. It appears that the rate of utilization of cloud computing services is increasing rapidly in Turkey. However, there are no laws protecting users against possible damages. This means that the risk of all data transferred to a cloud system is assumed by the user receiving cloud service.

Cloud computing is classified under four groups according to type of use. "Public Cloud" generating services (for example, Google Apps, Amazon, Windows Azure)

J.N. Gathegi et al. (Eds.): IMCW 2013, CCIS 423, pp. 36–42, 2014.

for general use on the Internet and via web interface, "Private Cloud" composed of cloud services provided for a certain body or institution, "Hybrid Cloud" generating public and private cloud services together, and "Community Cloud" provided for a specific community or group. Cloud computing service providers use software, platform and infrastructure service models, individually or in combination, in providing cloud service. In this study, terms of service of free cloud service providers that are globally outstanding in terms of widespread use of their e-mail and data storage services (such as Google, Microsoft and Yahoo) [3] are evaluated.

2   Cloud Computing: Problems and Risks

It is possible to access information anywhere with any kind of communication device (PC, Mac, iPhone, Android or BlackBerry) thanks to cloud computing. Cloud computing brings advantages to the user right from the outset: It does not present hardware problems; it provides better accessibility because virtual computers operate faster than physical servers, and also presents a flexible structure that does not require memory and disk change. Given the advantages, it would seem unreasonable to avoid cloud computing and insist on adopting alternative computing models. However, risks of cloud computing are highly important to the extent that they cannot be ignored. Terms of service are prepared for the benefit of the service provider only as they are not based on any legal regulation [4]. Main issues of concern that arise from cloud computing include:

- Web-based cloud services are designed to operate on broadband Internet. Therefore, downloading and uploading speed of the Internet connection is considerably important for using cloud services. About 43.2% of residences have broadband Internet access in Turkey [5]. Although Internet use and broadband Internet access are on the rise in Turkey, it can be safely said that, compared to EU countries, there still exists a considerable gap in this regard [6].

- There are also risks regarding protecting the privacy of user passwords and personal information at locations where users can have connection without even using a password (such as cafe, restaurant, bus etc.). As in all services based on Internet technology, there are vulnerabilities of cloud computing services against typical Internet attacks (such as electronic surveillance, unauthorized access, data modification etc.) [7].

- Details regarding the location of data are among the important issues that should be covered by the agreement signed between the user and the cloud computing services provider, and this could be useful in helping settle legal disputes in numerous countries, including Turkey. Nonetheless, many service providers offering free cloud service do not present the users the option of amendment on the agreement. It is clearly stated in the online privacy statement of such cloud service providers that personal information of the user can be stored and processed anywhere in the world (see, for example, Microsoft Online Privacy Statement) [8].

- Turkey does not have a binding regulation with regard to standards to be met in order to provide cloud computing service. Thus, an environment emerges where users can be aggrieved due to any number of reasons (such as termination of service, loss of data, privacy of personal data), because there is no legal regulation and supervision in terms of the qualifications of cloud computing service providers, such as adequate infrastructure, capital, and qualified personnel, among others).

- There may be interruptions in the services of large-scale companies including major cloud service providers such as Microsoft, Google, Yahoo, BlackBerry and Amazon [9]. However, cloud service providers do not bear any liability for the losses and return of information in the cloud system in the event of interruptions in services or termination of service by the provider (see, for example, Microsoft Online Privacy Statement) [8]. There is often no clarity in the agreements with regard to the duration of the waiting time for a system to be reactivated and to resume operating in the event of a disaster.

- Certain terms of service state that the service provider may use, change, adapt, record, recreate, distribute and monitor the content with the aim of improving its service quality (see, for example, Google Terms of Service or Microsoft Terms of Service) [10], [11]. Certain end-user license agreements (EULA have a statement stipulating that all license rights (right of duplication, transfer, publication and storing) are permanently assigned to the service provider (to provide services) [12]. It appears that the scope of authorization obtained by the service providers in order to provide their services is far too broad [13].

- During any investigation of digital evidence, data located in the same environment which is not related with the illegal act in question become accessible and files not related with any criminal offense are changed in structure, which may lead to the emergence of new legal problems. Furthermore, although some EULAs clearly state that deleted information may not at the same time be deleted from the information environments (see Google Privacy Policy) [14], there is no information available regarding when a complete deletion process might be accomplished.

3   Legal Liabilities of Cloud Service Providers

3.1   Legal Environment Regarding Cloud Computing in the USA

Unlike the EU, the US has no comprehensive law protecting the privacy of personal information and limiting the transfer of data to other countries. However, data that can be classified as sensitive is addressed in federal law, and certain limitations are imposed on such data because of the need for privacy [15]. Sensitive data include four domains: personal information collected from those under the age of 13, personal information collected by financial institutions about their clients, healthcare information collected by healthcare institutions about their patients, and information collected by the credit bureaus regarding the credit history of their clients.

Personal information collected in these four domains is to be used in the respective domain only and not to be revealed unlawfully. There are also various proposed legislative bills defining sensitive data such as health records, ethnic information, religious beliefs, sexual preferences, geographical and location information, financial information, biometric data and social security number of the users and accordingly, for the purposes of protecting personal information [16]. Federal regulations require companies to abide by minimum security rules and they incentivize them in this respect. For instance, healthcare institutions are obliged to provide for the security of personal healthcare information, yet they do not have to store information in an encrypted state. However, if the information is stored by encryption at an adequate level, institutions shall not be forced to publicly declare the fact that there has been an unauthorized access to information. Thereby, institutions will not be faced with unnecessary expenditures, customer attrition and loss of reputation. Thus, many healthcare institutions prefer data encryption. If a healthcare institution transfers patient information to a cloud system located in a different country and information security is violated on this system, then the cloud service provider is not deemed liable as per the US law and the provider holds liability only in the framework of the agreement between the provider and the user (while the health institution is still liable). Furthermore, such healthcare institution is obliged to declare the information security violation. Although there is not a uniform law on this issue, every state obliges companies within their borders to inform their users about security violations in the framework of "data breach notification statutes" [15]. There are penal sanctions for not abiding by these statutes.

3.2 Legal Environment Regarding Cloud Computing in EU and New Trends

EU has introduced legal regulations in various fields for the protection of personal data. Among them is Directive 95/46/EC. This is of utmost importance as it is the data protection directive in effect and lays the basis for the directive drafts prepared to respond to novel developments. Directive 95/46/EC clarifies the issues with regard to protection of fundamental rights of the users, limiting company processing of data (collecting, recording, using and disclosure of information), requiring minimal recording of personal information, and informing the user about data processing procedures [17]. The nature of cloud system entails user information to be located on the server (and maybe abroad, most of the times). However, Directive 95/46/EC prohibits the transfer of personal information outside the EU economic zone as long as data security is not maintained by the destination country. There is, however, an exemption created as per Decision 2000/520/EC of the European Commission dated 26 July 2000 formulated in accordance with the Directive 95/46/EC. The exemption creates a "Safe Harbour" for companies transferring information from EU to the USA [18].

Since 2009, the EU Commission has been exerting more effort in terms of reviewing the definition and the scope of EU data protection law and privacy of personal data. "Strategy on Protecting Personal Data" published on 4 November 2010 (reference no IP/10/1462) and memorandum MEMO/10/542 are important documents that provide an idea about the reforms to be introduced in data protection law

95/46/EC. Statements were made during the sessions organized by the EU Commission in January 2012 that the main obstacle in the path of the use of cloud computing are worries about the data protection arising from the data protection laws varying from country to country within EU, and that it was important that EU Council and Parliament work on a new regulation as soon as possible. The current data protection directive, 95/46/EC, falls short and/or bears uncertainties in terms of using and providing new Internet services (cloud computing, social networking web sites etc.) and this has led to the preparation of a new personal data protection draft directive (reference no IP/12/46), which is a comprehensive reform in the data protection law, on the basis of the preliminary projects started in 2010 [19]. This new personal data protection draft, which includes reforms regarding possible risks of cloud computing, was submitted for the approval of the EU Council and Parliament on 25 January 2012. Topics related to cloud computing include: transfer of personal data between service providers, clarification of the conditions under which personal data can be obtained, "right to be forgotten" enabling a data subject to manage her/his online data protection rights, informing a data subject at every stage of data processing, including information about any security violations during the process [20].

3.3   Laws Regarding Cloud Computing in Turkey

As there is no law regarding the privacy of personal information and data protection in cloud computing, the relationship between service providers and users is limited to terms of service agreements and there is little legal recourse for the user in resolving disputes stemming from the relationship with the service provider. The issue of personal information privacy in general is addressed in Article 20 in the Turkish Constitution (with the Annex in 2010) [21] and Article 135 and 136 in the Turkish Penal Code (TPC) [22] within Turkish legislation. However, it is evident that the regulations in the Constitution and TPC are not even at the protection level of data protection law which has been in force within EU since 1998 and which is already thought to be insufficient in the presence of new technologies. A choice of law or choice of forum that specifies jurisdiction outside the borders of Turkey in the terms of service means that an international and excessively costly legal struggle will be required in order to submit a claim in the event of a dispute. In the event that choice of law (jurisdiction) is not mentioned in the terms of service and servers of the service provider are located in a different country; Article 12 and 13 of TPC [22], to which individuals may think of referring, remain incapable of providing relief in the context of cloud computing. Article 12 of TPC, which is based on the principle of protection of the injured party in the event of criminal acts committed outside Turkey, stipulates that the offender, who commits the illegal act abroad, should be within the borders of Turkey. Other illegal acts committed abroad are mentioned in Article 13 of TPC. However, Article 13 is far from being a settling article in terms of disputes about cloud as cybercrimes are not included in the catalogue of crimes addressed in this Article.

Turkey is a party to important conventions established by the European Council in order to protect personal information and individual rights. None of them, however, have been put into effect by harmonizing them with the domestic law. Passing the "Motion for Personal Data Protection", which will harmonize the Convention with the domestic law, is necessary in order that the Convention no. 108 (the first regulation within the international law on data protection) signed by Turkey on 28 January 1981 be approved. Additional Protocol no 181 (Protocol regarding Supervisory Authorities and Transborder Data Flow), which is highly related to cloud computing services, was signed by Turkey on 8 November 2001 but has not yet been approved for domestic law. One of the most important legal documents prepared by the European Commission with regard to international cybercrimes is Convention on Cybercrime no 185 [23]. Prepared with the contributions of the USA and opened for signature on 23 November 2001, Convention on Cybercrime no 185 was signed by Turkey on 10 November 2010. However, Convention on Cybercrime could not be put into effect either for lack of the required regulations in domestic law.

4   Conclusion

Numerous risks exist for the users receiving service via cloud computing, particularly with regard to data protection. While it is regarded as normal to experience certain problems in the launching period of a new technology, it is highly important to raise the awareness of the users at the optimum stage in order to minimize adverse effects. Cloud computing is regarded as the focal spot where information and computer technologies are heading towards. But on the other hand, problems of cloud computing have been scrutinized along with the benefits and accordingly, a number of policies and projects with regard to data security have been introduced by the EU and the USA. However, it is also observed that EU and the US laws on privacy and security have been reviewed in order to provide adequate protection for the sensitive data belonging to users.

Cloud computing is situated within an excessively broad scope of legal liability. The concept of personal data protection, which is being protected by the federal law in the USA and covered by a certain framework through the Convention No. 108 of the European Council and the Additional Protocol No. 181, is still far from the attention and the agenda of Turkey in terms of its legal dimension. This study observed that legal infrastructure with regard to protection of data and personal information has not been established yet and users are left to take measures and responsibility for data security within the cyber environment, on their own. Although Turkey is a party to numerous missions and conventions initiated by EU (such as the Conventions No. 108 and 185 etc.), these initiatives cannot be put into effect due to the lack of the required regulations in the domestic law. Required regulations are needed in order to apply to cloud services in Turkey the articles regarding data security, which are included in the terms of services of cloud computing but as of yet cover only the users from certain countries (such as USA, Australia, European Economic Area and Switzerland etc.).

References

1. European Commission: Unleashing the Potential of Cloud Computing in Europe, http://ec.europa.eu/information_society/activities/cloudcomputing/docs/com/com_cloud.pdf

2. Paquette, S., Jaeger, P., Wilson, S.: Identifying the Security Risks Associated with Governmental Use of Cloud Computing. Government Information Quarterly 27, 245–253 (2010)
3. Kaufman, L.: Data Security in the World of Cloud Computing. IEEE Computer and Reliability Societies 7, 61–64 (2009)
4. Wyld, D.C.: Moving to the Cloud: An Introduction to Cloud Computing in Government, http://faculty.cbpp.uaa.alaska.edu/afgjp/PADM601%20Fall%2020 10/Moving%20to%20the%20Cloud.pdf
5. TÜİK: Hanehalkı Bilişim Teknolojileri Kullanım Araştırması. Türkiye İstatistik Kurumu, Ankara (2012)
6. DPT: Bilgi Toplumu İstatistikleri - 2011. T.C. Başbakanlık Devlet Planlama Teşkilatı, Ankara (2011)
7. Bisong, A., Rahman, S.: An Overview of the Security Concerns in Enterprise Cloud Computing. International Journal of Network Security & Its Applications (IJNSA) 3(1), 30–45 (2011)
8. Microsoft: Microsoft Online Privacy Statement, http://privacy.microsoft.com /TR-TR/fullnotice.mspx
9. Perlin, M.: Downtime, Outages and Failures - Understanding Their True Costs, http:// www.evolven.com/blog/downtime-outages-and-failures- understanding-their-true-costs.html
10. Google: Google Hizmet Şartları, http://www.google.com/policies/terms/
11. Microsoft: Microsoft Hizmetler Sözleşmesi, http://windows.microsoft.com/tr -TR/windows-live/microsoft-services-agreement
12. Acer Inc.: AcerCloud Son Kullanıcı Lisans Sözleşmesi, https://www.cloud.acer. com/ops/showEula
13. Svantesson, D., Clarke, R.: Privacy and Consumer Risks in Cloud Computing. Computer Law & Security Review 26, 391–397 (2010)
14. Google: Gizlilik Politikası, http://www.google.com/policies/privacy/
15. King, N.J., Raja, V.: Protecting the Privacy and Security of Sensitive Customer Data in the Cloud. Computer Law & Security Review 28, 308–319 (2012)
16. U.S.C.: In the House of Representatives, http://www.gpo.gov/fdsys/pkg/ BILLS-112hr611ih/pdf/BILLS-112hr611ih.pdf
17. European Council: Directive 95/46/EC of the European Parliament and of the Council, http://idpc.gov.mt/dbfile.aspx/Directive%2095-46%20- %20Part%202.pdf
18. European Commission: Commission Staff Working Document, http://ec.europa. eu/justice/policies/privacy/docs/adequacy/sec-2004- 1323_en.pdf
19. European Commission: Commission proposes a comprehensive reform of the data protection rules, http://ec.europa.eu/justice/newsroom/ data-protection/news/120125_en.htm
20. European Commission: How does the Data Protection Reform Strengthen Citizens' Rights?, http://ec.europa.eu/justice/data-protection/ document/review2012/factsheets/2_en.pdf
21. Anayasası, T.C.: Türkiye Cumhuriyeti Anayasası, http://www.tbmm.gov.tr/ anayasa/anayasa_2011.pdf
22. Türk Ceza Kanunu, http://www.tbmm.gov.tr/kanunlar/k5237.html
23. European Commission. Convention on Cybercrime, http://conventions.coe. int/treaty/en/treaties/html/185.htm

Trustworthy Digital Images and the Cloud: Early Findings of the Records in the Cloud Project

Jessica Bushey

GRA, Records in the Cloud Project, iSchool @UBC,
Vancouver, British Columbia, Canada
`jbushey@mail.ubc.ca`

Abstract. Digitized and born digital images are being created and disseminated at an ever-increasing rate as the by-products of business activities and the residue of organizational culture. In the past decade, the popularity of digitization as an archival activity aimed at preserving vulnerable archival materials and providing increased access to archival collections has presented archivists with a number of challenges including: platform interoperability, access controls, scalable infrastructure and privacy and rights management. The Cloud presents a range of solutions to the problems posed by managing large data sets such as digital image collections; however, at this early stage the benefits and risks associated with cloud-based services are still being identified. This paper will discuss the current state of digital imaging and highlight key issues in the creation and use, management, and preservation of digital images as trustworthy records in the context of an evolving online environment.

Keywords: Digital images, archives, cloud computing, trustworthy records.

1 Introduction

The broad theme of the 4th International Symposium on Information Management in a Changing World (IMCW2013) is the role of Cloud Computing in current information management issues. This paper discusses the current state of digital imaging in individual and organizational contexts and highlights the key issues in the creation, use, management and preservation of trustworthy digital images in commercial online environments. Emphasis will be placed on the role of the information professional in the digital era and key factors for and against adoption of cloud-based services by organizations (including archival institutions) for storing and accessing their collections of digital images. The author is a graduate research assistant with three projects, in which digital records management and preservation in the online environment are being explored: Records in the Cloud (RIC) (<http://www.recordsinthecloud.org>), the Law of Evidence in the Digital Environment (LEDE) (<http://www.lawofevidence.org>), and InterPARES Trust (<http://www.interparestrust.org>).

This paper focuses on the RIC project, which is a 4-year international research collaboration between the University of British Columbia (UBC) School of Library, Archival and Information Studies (SLAIS), the Faculty of Law, and the Sauder

J.N. Gathegi et al. (Eds.): IMCW 2013, CCIS 423, pp. 43–53, 2014.

School of Business; the University of Washington School of Information; the University of North Carolina at Chapel Hill School of Information and Library Science; the Mid-Sweden University Department of Information Technology and Media; the University of Applied Sciences of Western Switzerland School of Business Administration; and the Cloud Security Alliance [1]. The RIC research addresses the growing number of individuals, and public and private organizations that are adopting cloud-based services, in an effort to save resources, without exploring the full extent of the benefits and risks posed by entrusting the control of their records to external service providers. The current lack of academic research into accessing and storing records in the cloud, combined with the nascence of these services to individuals and organizations, makes this study both necessary and urgent. The potential for cloud providers to change their services, go bankrupt, or be purchased by another provider presents the opportunity for records to be lost, altered, or deleted. For individuals and organizations delegating responsibility for the ongoing access and long-term preservation of their records to cloud-service providers, these are serious concerns. Lastly, cloud-based services introduce a degree of complexity that impacts many areas, including privacy, intellectual property and e-discovery.

Utilizing the theoretical constructs of archival science and diplomatics (i.e., the study of the genesis, form and transmission of documents in order to establish their authenticity and reliability) and the concepts developed by the International Research on Permanent Authentic Records in Electronic Systems (InterPARES) Projects 1, 2, 3 (<http://www.interpares.org>) and the Digital Records Forensics (<http://www.digitalrecordsforensics.org>) Project, the RIC research will investigate the following questions:

- How can confidentiality of organizational records and data privacy be protected in the cloud?
- How can forensic readiness of an organization be maintained, compliance ensured, and e-discovery requests fully met in the cloud?
- How can an organization's records accuracy, reliability, and authenticity be guaranteed and verifiable in the cloud?
- How can an organization's records and information security be enforced in the cloud?
- How can an organization maintain governance upon the records entrusted in the cloud?

Early RIC research activities include a literature review, an online survey of cloud-service users and potential users, and interviews with cloud-service providers. Informed by the products of these research activities, this paper will discuss the trustworthiness of digital photographs in the cloud.

1.1   Background and Context

In the past decade, one focus of archival institutions has been on digitizing archival holdings for the purposes of increasing access to their holdings and supporting the preservation of fragile media, such as photographs in glass plate format or unstable moving image film. Traditional photographic media is comprised of layers of materials and combinations of chemicals that are highly susceptible to deterioration in the presence of light, heat and moisture. Digitization of photographic media through scanning and migration has enabled archivists to expose collections for discovery and use to a larger audience while supporting the long-term preservation of the original records (e.g., glass lantern slides, film-based negatives, silver gelatin prints etc.). The standards that guide digitization of still and moving images recommend the creation of preservation masters and reference copies for access and use, which inevitably results in the archival institution becoming responsible for managing and preserving the original record, the digital preservation master and the digital reference/access copies [2]. The proper management of digitized holdings requires software to provide access and a system to preserve the master files, in which migrations can be planned. Depending upon the size of the digital holdings, archival institutions implement strategies that incorporate on-site and/or off-site storage and backup, which remains under their control, or off-site storage and backup provided by a trusted third-party. Recent developments in cloud computing are introducing new opportunities to archival institutions interested in outsourcing the management and preservation of their digital resources to third-party providers.

The second focus of archival institutions has been on the acquisition of born-digital images. Since the early 1990s individuals and organizations have been creating digital records as by-products of business and personal activities. The records are typically accessed and stored on personal computers, external media such as compact discs (CD) and hard drives. A number of recommendations and guidelines aimed at helping creators and preservers ensure the long-term accessibility and readability of born-digital resources have been produced by research projects conducted by archivists and heritage professionals [3], [4], [5], [6], [7]. However, the recent convergence of cameras into mobile devices with Internet connectivity and photo-sharing and social networking sites that provide digital image access, management and storage presents a new level of complexity for information professionals charged with protecting and preserving digital images as reliable and authentic records for future use. Unlike personal computers and boxes of floppy discs, digital image collections held within online accounts and made available through photo-sharing and social networking platforms such as Flickr (<http://www.flickr.com>), Facebook (<http://www.facebook.com>) and Instagram (<http://www.instagram.com>) are part of a larger system that relies on cloud computing infrastructure to enable providers to manage vast data sets (e.g., millions of digital images) and deliver continuous and scalable services to customers. The workings of these systems are relatively unknown to many heritage professionals (e.g., archivists, curators, special collections librarians) and others who have entrusted their digital image collections to providers of cloud-based infrastructure and software services. Many of the commercial online services aimed at providing individuals and organizations with scalable solutions to storing and accessing volumes of digital assets are private for-profit companies utilizing proprietary technologies. The future sustainability of these companies is unknown and the legal agreements (i.e., Terms and Conditions) that define how user accounts and user-generated content is controlled, including policies for data protection and privacy, and copyright and intellectual property can be modified without notice to their customers [8].

To conclude this section, it is necessary to emphasize that digital images are created as business records in a number of contexts that require strict controls over the procedures of creation, management and preservation in order to ensure their trustworthiness. Archivists informed by archival science and diplomatics are committed to the protection of records as reliable and authentic evidence of past actions, and have established through observational principles that trustworthiness is comprised of reliability, accuracy, and authenticity; thus, a trustworthy photograph must be simultaneously reliable, accurate, and authentic [9]. If we want assurance of the trustworthiness of a photograph we need to verify that the photograph is capable of standing for the facts to which it attests (i.e., reliable), its content is precise, correct, and free of error or distortion (i.e., accurate), and that the photograph is what it purports to be and has not been corrupted or tampered with (i.e., authentic). Digital images created during the activities of law enforcement, journalism, medical diagnostics, and geospatial exploration are expected to be accurate, reliable and authentic in order to fulfill their intended purposes. Additionally, as more people live digital lives, future researchers will want assurance that the digital photographs and moving images they are consulting are trustworthy records and that the contexts in which they were created are preserved along with the content. Therefore, the benefits and risks of adopting cloud-based systems for digital image access, use and storage need to be explored by archivists using criteria informed by the principles of archival science and the application of contemporary archival diplomatics.

2   Methods

Prior to launching the web-based survey, an extensive literature review was conducted exploring key aspects of cloud computing, including infrastructure and architecture, security and privacy, copyright, and the legal admissibility of records held within the cloud. The literature review revealed articles in which individuals and organizations discuss the risks and benefits of adopting cloud computing for the healthcare industry (e.g., diagnostic images) [10], [11] and the records management and archives sector [12]. These articles focus on the benefits of cloud computing for dealing with high volumes of data (e.g., high resolution digital images), which require limitless storage and are accessed by users on a variety of mobile devices and platforms, twenty-four hours a day and seven days a week [10]. Furthermore, the multi-tenancy environment of some cloud services maximize computing and storage capacities, which provide computing resources at lower costs and enable flexible and scalable solutions for organizations that may not have in-house IT infrastructure [12]. Solutions provided by cloud computing reflect the changing needs of an increasingly mobile workforce that may work collaboratively within their organization, but are geographically dispersed and need access to shared digital resources in order to make decisions and deliver projects.

In April 2013, a short web-based survey was conducted under the auspices of the Records in the Cloud project [13]. Invitations to participate in the Cloud User Survey were sent to records managers, archival listservs and archival associations with the aim of gathering information about the types of cloud computing services being used by information professionals for records management and preservation. Following a pilot study with volunteer respondents, the revised survey questionnaire was launched on April 11, 2013. The questionnaire explored motivations and concerns about adopting cloud services as well as issues encountered in using cloud computing. A total of thirty-four questions were asked, with specific questions included to identify organizational-level understanding of cloud computing as opposed to individual impressions. Both closed and open-ended question types were used, which provided an opportunity for respondents to elaborate on their experiences. The online survey was available for approximately one month and 353 responses were collected. The completion rate was fifty percent. The majority of study respondents are located in North America; however, fifty-two countries are represented overall.

3   Results

The following results have been selected for their relevance to digital image practice, a review of the entire survey can be found in the "RIC User Survey Report" [13]. Over half the survey respondents work in organizations that use cloud computing (Fig. 1), and thirty-eight percent of the organizations that do not use cloud computing are currently considering adoption (Fig. 2).

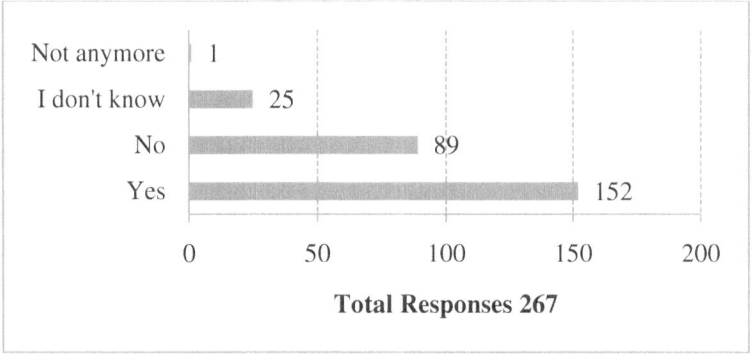

Fig. 1. Does your organization use cloud computing?

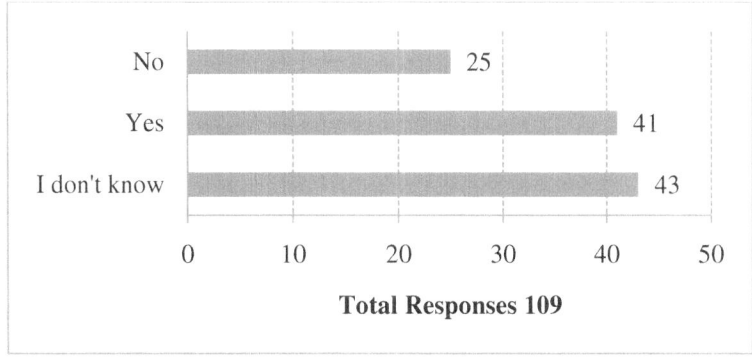

Fig. 2. Has your organization considered using cloud computing?

The primary reasons organizations use cloud computing are to reduce their costs, increase collaboration and increase their storage capacity (Fig. 3), with additional responses provided (i.e., other) that identified the ease of accessing files from multiple computing devices and by employees working remotely.

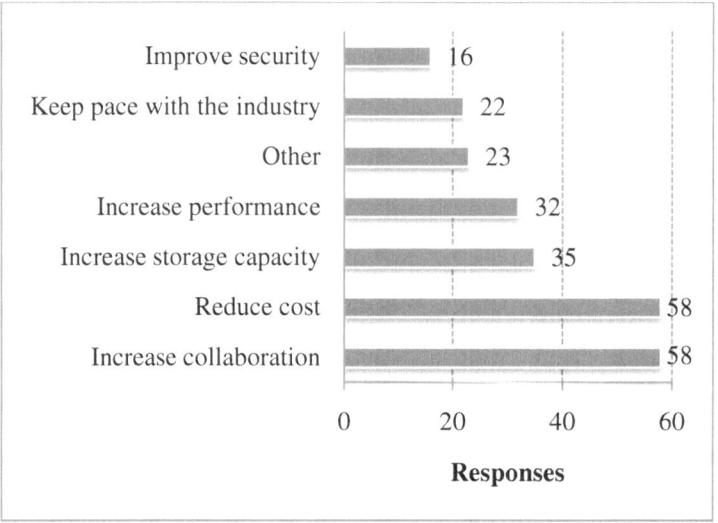

Fig. 3. What are the primary reasons your organization uses cloud computing? (Select all that apply)

In contrast, the primary reasons organizations do not use cloud computing are security risks, legal implications, loss of control over data, and privacy risks (Fig. 4).

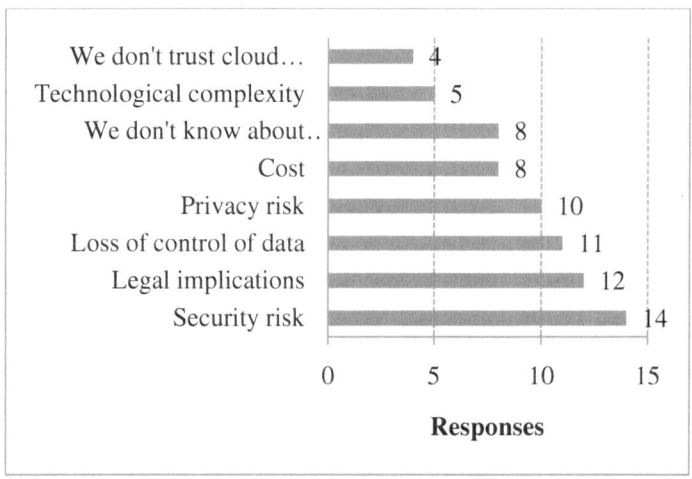

Fig. 4. Why is your organization not considering cloud computing? (Select all that apply)

All the organizations in the study that use cloud computing are utilizing the public cloud service model. Of these organizations, only a small percentage negotiated a service-level agreement (i.e., terms and conditions) with their provider (Fig. 5).

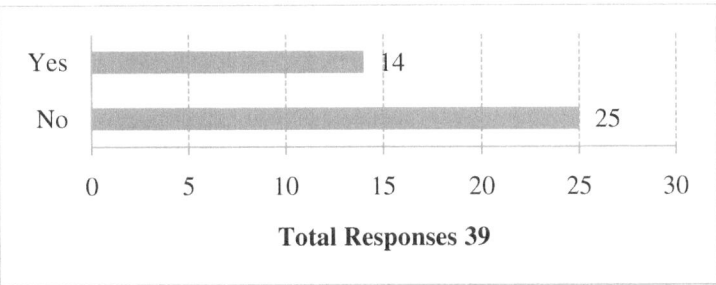

Fig. 5. Did your organization negotiate a service-level agreement rather than accepting the provider's standard agreement?

The organizations that did negotiate a service-level agreement with the cloud service provider prioritized ownership of data and metadata, backup and recovery, and the appropriateness of technology and security (Fig. 6).

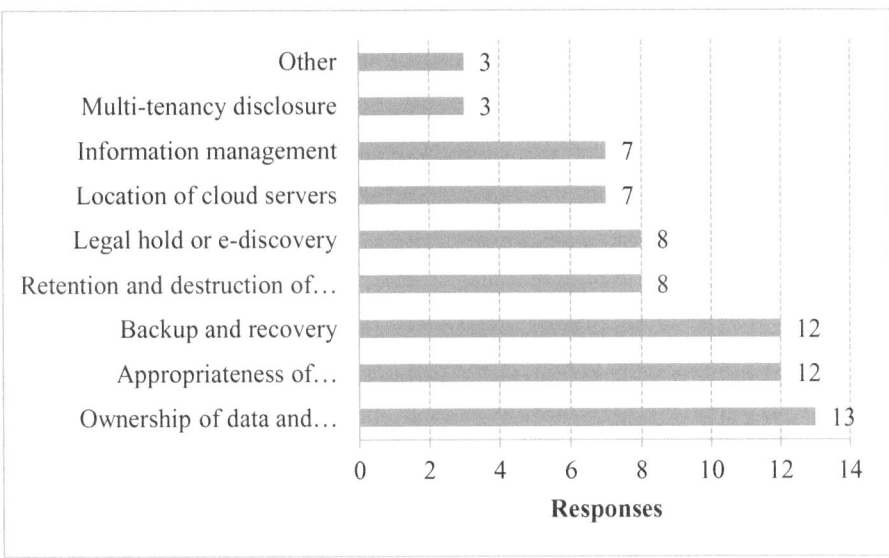

Fig. 6. When your organization negotiated a service-level agreement with the cloud service provider, which issues were important to your organization? (Select all that apply)

4   Early Findings and Discussion

The early findings of the Records in the Cloud User Survey reflect opinions expressed in the literature on cloud computing, mainly that adoption is being driven by perceived cost benefits and the needs of a changing workforce that access shared resources remotely on a variety of digital devices [14]. Organizations that allow mobile computing (i.e., any computing performed outside the office using smartphones and tablets) and rely on the public cloud model are exposing their organizational records to a number of threats, including unauthorized network access, data loss (e.g., stolen or lost devices), and a lack of management tools to control disposition and long-term preservation.

The concerns expressed by organizations that have yet to adopt cloud-based services share common ground with the issues raised by organizations when negotiating the service-level agreement with cloud providers. These concerns must be addressed at the outset, typically through service level agreements (SLA). The terms and conditions that form an integral part of the contract between cloud providers and customers can be complex and involve a hierarchy of agreements and policies in a set of documents including the terms of service, service level agreement, acceptable use policy, and privacy policy. An individual or organization that has an account with Instagram may not be aware that the site is a subsidiary of Facebook, who rents data storage and computer server time from *Amazon's* cloud computing service Amazon Web Services (<aws.amazon.com>), which has over 800,000 data servers dedicated to cloud computing in the Eastern United States, and additional data centers in the Western United States, Brazil, Ireland, Singapore, Sydney and Tokyo. In this example, there are multiple agreements between all parties, numerous jurisdictions in which the data flows throughout as it moves from data center to data center, and the opportunity for digital image files to be altered either accidentally or intentionally. SLA are the first and only place for the cloud customer to establish parameters for controlling information retrieval (i.e., access), complying with data protection acts, and determining legal custody of stored records. Unfortunately, for most individuals and many smaller organizations, SLA are not negotiable; yet, it is a contractual agreement and thus, legally binding.

The ownership and use of digital images held within the Instagram platform came under attack in late 2012 when the company changed the Terms of Service (ToS) to grant the photo-sharing site perpetual rights to all images uploaded to their site for the commercial purposes of Instagram [15]. The backlash from customers was noticeable and quickly spawned a number of articles discussing the ownership of digital photographs (and digital content in general) stored in the commercial online environment, and by extension, the rights of service providers vs. the rights of customers [16]. In response to public pressure the company withdrew the change in ToS.

The findings of the cloud user survey reveal that the minority of organizations that do negotiate SLA with cloud providers (Fig. 5) prioritize the ownership of data and metadata. In the context of digital image collections, the importance of metadata embedded in the image files, as well as metadata generated during activities of use, management, and preservation cannot be overemphasized. In 2004 the "Survey of the Recordkeeping Practices of Photographers using Digital Technology," conducted under the auspices of the International Research on Permanent Authentic Records in Electronic Systems: Experiential, Interactive and Dynamic Records Project

(InterPARES 2) revealed that professional photographers are aware of the role of metadata embedded in image files to identify the who, what, where, when and why, of the content and the context of the image-making event, along with important copyright information and licensing parameters [17]. This is typically achieved through the addition of technical metadata (e.g., Exif) and management metadata (e.g., IPTC Core) during the activities of image capture, use and storage. An authentic digital photograph possesses identity (i.e, the whole of the unique characteristics that distinguish it from another photograph), such as information about the date(s) of creation and transmission, name(s) of the photographer, camera make and model etc., and integrity (i.e., the quality of being whole and unaltered) [3], [4]. Integrity is protected through procedures exercising control over transmission and access. Unfortunately, the recent convergence of digital cameras into mobile phones, laptops and tablets with Internet connectivity to cloud based services has provided the tools and means for anyone to quickly create and store digital images; but, without the awareness or concern of professional photographers and information professionals for capturing metadata that contributes to record identity and integrity.

A recent study conducted by the Photo Metadata Working Group of the International Press Telecommunications Council (IPTC) investigates the risk of inadvertently deleting digital image metadata that contribute to record identity and integrity during the management and use of digital images on photo-sharing and social networking sites such as Facebook, Twitter (<https://twitter.com>), Dropbox (<https://www.dropbox.com>) and Flickr [18]. Their findings reveal that digital image metadata are inconsistently supported across social media sites and that the two most popular sites for sharing digital photographs, Flickr and Facebook remove metadata from the image file header during procedures for saving a digital photograph to a desktop and downloading a digital photograph using the menu controls provided in the social media user-interface. The results of this study were discussed in the United States Library of Congress "Signal Blog," expressing concern over the trove of visual heritage that is now being controlled by for-profit companies in the online environment [19]. From an information management perspective, the removal of metadata that contribute to the identity and integrity of the digital image, as well as metadata that inform future users about the copyright and usage of the image is highly problematic. Records managers and archivists that work with digital image collections, both digitized and born digital, need to revisit existing strategies for managing and preserving digital images as trustworthy records in light of new digital imaging practices and online platforms that rely on cloud computing services. Furthermore, archival institutions considering acquisition of digital image collections from organizations and individuals, which use cloud-based services for storage need to be aware that actions undertaken to download content out of the online platform may remove metadata that establishes the provenance of the digital image collection and its functional context. Additional challenges regarding the ownership of the user-generated content (i.e., the copyright may be held by the account holder but the platform provider has a license to use it) may need to be considered by archival institutions prior to acquisition.

In summary, the role of the information professional in the digital era is to understand and evaluate new methods of creating, managing and storing digital records (e.g., image, audio, video and text). As image-making practices evolve, both creators and preservers are adopting new technologies to assist in accessing, disseminating, managing and storing large data sets such as digital image collections. It is the responsibility of archivists and librarians to weigh the benefits and risks posed by proprietary cloud based solutions. It is important to remember that these solutions are not trusted digital preservation systems in which metadata is managed and generated throughout the lifecycle of the digital record. The lack of transparency and control provided by third-party services that utilize cloud-based infrastructure and services present a number of challenges to determining what is actually happening to the digital information held within these systems. At this stage there are many issues to explore and few guidelines to assist individuals and organizations in selecting cloud based services [12]. The outcome of international multidisciplinary projects such as Records in the Cloud, the Law of Evidence in the Digital Environment and InterPARES Trust will be the contribution of research findings towards the development of international policies, procedures and standards concerning digital records entrusted to the Internet.

Acknowledgments. The Records in the Cloud (RIC) Project is supported by a Social Sciences and Humanities Research Council of Canada (SSHRC) Insight Grant.

References

1. Records in the Cloud Project (2012-2016), http://www.recordsinthecloud.org/
2. Federal Agencies Digitization Initiative – Still Image Working Group: Technical Guidelines for Digitizing Cultural Heritage Materials: Creation of Raster Image Master Files. Technical Guidelines, FADGI (2010), http://www.digitizationguidelines.gov/guidelines/digitize-technical.html
3. Duranti, L., Preston, R.: Creator Guidelines, Making and Maintaining Digital Materials: Guidelines for Individuals. InterPARES 2 Project (2008), http://www.interpares.org/public_documents/ip2pubcreator_guidelines_booklet.pdf
4. Duranti, L., Preston, R.: Preserver Guidelines, Preserving Digital Records: Guidelines for Organizations. InterPARES 2 Project (2008), http://www.interpares.org/public_documents/ip2pubpreserver_guidelines_booklet.pdf
5. Thomas, S. (ed.): Workbook on Digital Private Papers. PARADIGM (2008), http://www.paradigm.ac.uk/workbook/index.html
6. Lee, C. (ed.): I, Digital: Personal Collections in the Digital Era. Society of American Archivists, Chicago (2011)
7. John, J.L., Rowlands, I., Williams, P., Dean, K.: Digital Lives. Personal Digital Archives for the 21st Century > >An Initial Synthesis, Digital Lives Research paper, Beta Version 0.2. The British Library (2010), http://britishlibrary.typepad.co.uk/files/digital-lives-syntesis01-1.pdf
8. Instagram. Terms of Use (2013), http://instagram.com/about/legal/terms/
9. InterPARES Project. Terminology, http://www.interpares.org/ip2/ip2_terminology_db.cfm

10. Shrestha, R.B.: Imaging on the Cloud. Applied Radiology 50, 8–12 (2011)
11. AT&T. Medical Imaging in the Cloud. White Paper (2012), `http://www.corp.att.com/healthcare/docs/medical_imaging_cloud.pdf`
12. Convery, N.: Cloud Computing Toolkit: Guidance for Outsourcing Information Storage to the Cloud. Archives & Records Association, UK & Ireland (2010), `http://www.archives.org.uk/images/documents/Cloud_Computing_Toolkit-2.pdf`
13. Duranti, L., Weimei, P., Rowe, J., Barlaoura, G., UBC, SLAIS.: Records in the Cloud (RIC) User Survey Report, V.10.1. Records in the Cloud Project (2013), `http://www.recordsinthecloud.org/assets/documents/RiC_Oct232013_User_Survey_Report.pdf`
14. Cloud Security Alliance Mobile Working Group: Security Guidance for Critical Areas of Mobile Computing, V.1.0. Cloud Security Alliance (2012), `https://downloads.cloudsecurityalliance.org/initiatives/mobile/Mobile_Guideance_v1.pdf`
15. ASMP: The Instagram Papers. ASMP (2013), `http://asmp.org/articles/press-release-13-08-22.html#.Uig3oGSzymA`
16. Rushton, K.: Instagram Battles against Rules Backlash. The Telegraph, Telegraph Media Group (December 19, 2012), `http://www.telegraph.co.uk/finance/newsbysector/mediatechnologyandtelecoms/digital-media/9756462/Instagram-battles-against-rules-backlash.html`
17. Bushey, J., Braun, M.: General Study 07 Final Report: Survey of Recordkeeping Practices of Photographers using Digital Technology. InterPARES 2 Project (2006), `http://www.interpares.org/display_file.cfm?doc=ip2_gs07_final_report.pdf`
18. IPTC Metadata Working Group: Social Media Sites: Photo Metadata Test Results (2013), `http://www.embeddedmetadata.org/social-media-test-results.php`
19. Riecks, D.: Social Media Networks Stripping Data from Your Digital Photos. The Signal Digital Preservation Blog (2013), `http://blogs.loc.gov/digitalpreservation/2013/04/social-media-networks-stripping-data-from-your-digital-photos/`

Cloud Computing and Copyright: New Challenges in Legal Protection?

Mariliana Rico

Universidad Católica del Táchira, Calle 14 con Carrera 14, Edif. UCAT, San Cristóbal,
Táchira, Venezuela
mariliana@ricocarrillo.com

Abstract. This paper addresses the implications of cloud computing in copyrighted works under the USA Copyright Act provisions and court rulings, in order to determine the liability of cloud computing Service Providers for copyright infringement, and whether the current Law is able to address copyright issues in the cloud. To fulfill the main objective, and to understand legal implications, cloud computing technology and services are analyzed in the first part. The second part explores copyright legal protection and ISP liability for copyright infringement, and the different court rulings on liability related to copyright infringements on the Internet and in the cloud. The research is concluded with some considerations about the adequacy of current law to resolve copyright issues arising from cloud computing.

Keywords: Cloud computing, copyright, internet service providers, liability.

1 Introduction

Cloud computing services represent a new reality in the information society which has some implications for intellectual property, most of all in copyrighted works. The growth of cloud computing technology allows Internet users to access and store all manner of content, some of it copyrighted, in cloud/hosting servers located in various places, including internationally. Some of this content may be copyrighted.

The main concern with cloud computing services with regard to copyright is whether the law is able to address copyright issues arising from this technology. Once again, liability of Internet Services Providers (ISP) has been under examination by different courts in the USA, after legal actions seeking for liability of ISPs as contributors to copyright infringement.

This work will address the implications of cloud computing in copyrighted works under the Digital Millennium Copyright Act and USA court rulings, in order to determine a possible secondary liability of cloud computing service providers in copyright infringement, and whether the current law is able to address copyright issues in the cloud. Part I describes cloud computing technology and services. Part II explores copyright legal protection and ISP liability for copyright infringement. Part III analyzes the different court rulings addressing liability related to copyright

J.N. Gathegi et al. (Eds.): IMCW 2013, CCIS 423, pp. 54–63, 2014.
© Springer-Verlag Berlin Heidelberg 2014

infringements on the Internet and in the cloud. Part IV (Conclusion) answers the question about the adequacy of current law to resolve copyright issues arising from cloud computing.

2   Cloud Computing: Technical Basis and Legal Issues

In order to get a better comprehension of copyright issues in cloud computing, it is necessary to explore the technical foundations of this new technology. According to the National Institute of Standards and Technology (NIST):

> Cloud computing is a model for enabling convenient, on-demand network access to a shared pool of configurable computing resources (e.g. networks, servers, storage, applications, and services) that can be rapidly provisioned and released with minimal management effort or service provider interaction. This cloud model promotes availability and is composed of five essential characteristics, three service models, and four deployments models [1].

2.1   Essential Characteristics

According to NIST [1], the essential characteristics of the cloud are the following: On-demand self-service, broad network access, resource pooling, rapid elasticity, and measured service. Regarding copyright issues in cloud computing, on-demand self-service and broad network access are the most important.

On-demand self-service allows users to unilaterally provision computing capabilities, such as server time and network storage, as needed automatically without requiring human interaction with each service provider.

Broad network access means that capabilities are available over the network and accessed through standard mechanisms that promote use by heterogeneous thin or thick client platforms (e.g., mobile phones, tablets, laptops, and workstations).

Resource pooling allows multiple consumers to use a multi-tenant model, with different physical and virtual resources assigned and reassigned according to consumer demand.

Rapid elasticity means that capabilities can be provisioned and released to scale rapidly outward and inward commensurate with demand. This feature is important to consumers because the capabilities available for provisioning often appear to be unlimited and can be appropriate in any quantity and in any time.

Measured service means that cloud systems automatically control and optimize resource use by levering a metering capability at some level of abstraction appropriate to the type of service (e.g., storage, processing, bandwidth, and active user accounts). Resource usage can be monitored, controlled, and reported, providing transparency for both the provider and consumer of the utilized service.

2.2   Deployment Models

NIST defines four "deployment models": private cloud, community cloud, public cloud, and hybrid cloud. The differences between these models are important in copyright scope in order to determine liability for copyright infringement and effectiveness of current law in this field.

a) Private cloud. This cloud infrastructure is provisioned for exclusive use by a single organization comprising multiple consumers (e.g., business units). It may be owned, managed, and operated by the organization, a third party, or some combination of them, and it may exist on or off the premises.

b) Community cloud. This cloud infrastructure is provisioned for exclusive use by a specific community of consumers from organizations that have shared concerns (e.g., mission, security requirements, policy, and compliance considerations). It may be owned, managed, and operated by one or more of the organizations in the community, a third party, or some combination of them, and it may exist on or off the premises.

c) Public cloud. This cloud infrastructure is provisioned for open use by the general public. It may be owned, managed, and operated by a business, academic, or government organization, or some combination of them. It exists on the premises of the cloud provider.

d) Hybrid cloud. This cloud infrastructure is a composition of two or more distinct cloud infrastructures (private, community, or public) that remain unique entities, but are bound together by standardized or proprietary technology that enables data and application portability (e.g., cloud bursting for load balancing between clouds)

2.3   Legal Issues

The main legal issues in cloud computing are regarding copyright infringement liability, data protection, data portability, intellectual property, applicable law, and issues relating to cloud computing agreements. Following the main objective of this paper, we address the implications of cloud computing in copyrighted works, in order to determine the liability of cloud computing service providers for copyright infringement.

3   The Impact of New Technologies on Copyright Protection

3.1   The Sony Doctrine

New technologies have made an impact on copyright protection in different ways. One of the most renowned cases related to this matter is *Sony Corp. of America v. Universal City Studio*, also known as the "Betamax Case". This was the first time the Supreme Court analyzed the indirect liability of a new technology company in copyright infringement. In this case, the Court determined that even though some consumers used this technology for illicit purposes, others used it for "time shifting", recording and watching their favorite shows at a later time. The Court stated:

> …the sale of copying equipment, like the sale of other articles of commerce, does not constitute contributory infringement if the product is widely used for legitimate, unobjectionable purposes. Indeed, it need merely be capable of substantial non-infringing uses.

Sony doctrine is based on fair use of copyrighted material, and is considered the most important decision to balance the interest of copyright industries, creative information technology developers, and users of information technology. In this case, the Supreme Court adopted a solution that weighed the value and legitimacy of the new technology against the likely harm to copyright holders [2].

Nowadays, the Sony doctrine is used to deal with Internet Service Providers' liability, in order to determine a possible indirect liability for copyright infringements by the users of new technologies like P2P.

3.2   Internet and Intellectual Property

The impact of the Internet on intellectual property was addressed in 1996 by the World Intellectual Property Organization (WIPO) with two new treaties: the WIPO Copyright Treaty (WCT) and the WIPO Performances and Phonograms Treaty (WPPT) [3]. These treaties, known as "Internet Treaties", were approved with the purpose of updating the international treaties on copyright and related rights to the digital era, and provide additional protections for copyright holders derived from advancements in Information Technology.

3.3   Copyright Legal Protection in USA

In USA, copyright is protected under the Copyright Act of 1976, included in Title 17 of United States Code. In 2000, the Digital Millennium Copyright Act (DMCA) was approved. This Act is a consequence of Internet development, and implements the principles of WIPO treaties in this country. The USA Copyright Act was amended to incorporate the DMCA.

The DMCA establishes the safe harbor defense rules as a limitation of liability for ISP regarding copyright infringement by Internet users. The DMCA seeks to balance the interest of copyright owners and online service providers "…by promoting cooperation, minimizing copyright infringement, and providing a higher degree of certainty to service providers on the question of copyright infringement" (*Capitol Records, Inc. v. MP3tunes, LLC.*)

The Copyright Act also establishes the fair use exemptions in copyrighted works. The fair use of a copyrighted work is based on the purposes and character of the use, among other factors.

The safe harbor principles and fair use have been considered by courts in this country to determine ISP secondary liability for user services copyright infringements.

4   Intermediary Liability for Copyright Infringement

Intermediary liability for copyright infringement is determined by secondary liability doctrine, and safe harbor principles. Although some end users of certain technology may infringe copyright, it is necessary to determine the indirect intermediary liability.

4.1   Secondary Liability Doctrine

Before addressing ISP liability for copyright infringement, it is important to mention that to find an ISP liable for secondary liability, there has to be a primary liability. On the Internet, users have primary liability for uploading and making available copyrighted works to the public without authorization. Due to network configuration and users privacy, it is sometimes very difficult to find the primary person liable.

In the USA there are two different theories of secondary liability: vicarious liability and contributory infringement [4]. Vicarious liability is considered a form of indirect copyright infringement, and is applicable when the ISP has the ability to control users, and a direct financial benefit from allowing them to use copyrighted works without the author's authorization.

Contributory infringement is related to a party that, with knowledge of the infringing activity, induces, causes or materially contributes to the infringing conduct of another.

4.2   Safe Harbor

The DMCA's principal innovation in the field of copyright is the exemption from direct and indirect liability of Internet service providers. The DMCA created safe harbor provisions to protect service providers from copyright infringement liability based on certain common industry practices. With the DMCA safe harbors, Congress intended to provide clear liability rules for online service providers, and to promote cooperation between the content and technology industries in combating infringement online [2].

Section 512 of the U.S. Copyright Act refers to limitations of liability with regards to online content, and establishes the safe harbor principles as an exemption to ISP liability for copyright infringement. In order to establish these exemptions, section 512 differentiates between four kinds of activities of service providers: (a) transitory digital network communications, (b) system caching, (c) hosting information posted by users in their systems or networks; and (d) providing information location tools that may direct users to infringing material.

The first safe harbor refers to ISPs that provide transmission, routing and connection services. The second safe harbor refers to those who provide intermediate and temporary storage of material on any system or network. The third safe harbor refers to those who provide hosting services. The last safe harbor is related to those who are referring or linking users to an online location; search engines are included in this category.

The third DMCA safe harbor, which governs information residing on systems or networks at the directions of users, is applicable to cloud services. According to 512 (c) Section:

> A service provider shall not be liable for monetary relief, or, except as provided in subsection (j), for injunctive or other equitable relief, for infringement of copyright by reason of the provider's transmitting, routing, or providing connections for, material through a system or network controlled or operated by or for the service provider, or by reason of the intermediate and transient storage of that material in the course of such transmitting, routing, or providing connections, if the service provider
>
> (A)(i) does not have actual knowledge that the material or an activity using the material on the system or network is infringing;
> (ii) in the absence of such actual knowledge, is not aware of facts or circumstances from which infringing activity is apparent; or
> (iii) upon obtaining such knowledge or awareness, acts expeditiously to remove, or disable access to, the material;
> (B) does not receive a financial benefit directly attributable to the infringing activity, in a case in which the service provider has the right and ability to control such activity; and
> (C) upon notification of claimed infringement as described in paragraph (3), responds expeditiously to remove, or disable access to, the material that is claimed to be infringing or to be the subject of infringing activity

The ISPs can benefit from the safe harbor principles when they comply with the conditions provisioned under section 512 (i):

> i) Conditions for eligibility
> (1) Accommodation of technology. - The limitations on liability established by this section shall apply to a service provider only if the service provider
> (A) has adopted and reasonably implemented, and informed subscribers and account holders of the service provider's system or network of, a policy that provides for the termination in appropriate circumstances of subscribers and account holders of the service provider's system or network who are repeat infringers; and
>
> (B) accommodates and does not interfere with standard technical measures.

The limitations on liability established in this subsection apply to a service provider only if the service provider has designated an agent to receive notifications of claimed infringement (takedown notices). This is considered the most effective way established in the DMCA to protect copyright holders. This notification must be a written communication provided to the designated agent of a service provider, and include the elements described in the DMCA. Basically, the DMCA refers to the identification of the material that is claimed to be infringing or to be the subject of infringing activity and that is to be removed or access to which is to be disabled, and information reasonably sufficient to permit the service provider to locate the material.

When a service provider receives a notice of copyright infringement, it must remove or disable access to that material. This duty offers copyright holders an expedient remedy for individual instances of infringement, but because copyright holders bear the burden of monitoring user activity for infringement, takedown notices are effective only when user activity is public [2].

4.3   Fair Use

Section 107 of the U.S. Copyright Act establishes the fair use doctrine as an exemption of copyright protection. The fair use of a copyrighted work is based on the purpose and character of the use, and includes the use by reproduction in copies or phonorecords for purposes such as criticism, comment, news reporting, teaching (including multiple copies for classroom use), scholarship, or research. The following factors are to be considered to determine fair use:

- the purpose and character of the use;
- the nature of the copyrighted work;
- the amount and substantiality of the portion used in relation to the copyrighted work as a whole; and
- the effect of the use upon the potential market for or value of the copyrighted work.

These four fair use factors have to be considered on a case by case basis in order to determine if the use of copyrighted material without authorization is fair according to the statute, and are also applicable to uses from new technologies, including cloud computing services. Different courts have applied fair use analysis regarding ISP liability for copyright infringement. Fair use is considered a flexible doctrine that has evolved with the development of new technologies.

Even though users have the primary liability for copyright infringement, the ISP could be found indirectly liable. Fair use as an exemption of copyright is extended to ISP liability. If the user is using copyright material under any of the exemptions that are considered fair use, the ISP cannot be found liable in this matter. Fair use works at the periphery of copyright enforcement in the cloud, for it is an exception to the primary act of infringement and not a separate defense against secondary liability infringement claims [5].

5   File Sharing and Copyright Infringement

Before the development of cloud computing, the most important cases related to ISP secondary liability were connected to file sharing and Peer to Peer (P2P).

P2P technologies are distributed systems for sharing files online. Widespread use of computers and the Internet have reduced the cost of distributing entertainment media and increased the access to content distribution channel. P2P allows users to access and download copyrighted works (books, music, movies) without the author's consent. By using specialized software, users are able to share these files.

P2P became popular in 1999 with the introduction of Napster, a central application which allowed users to share files. Napster was sued for copyright infringement, and the court found the corporation liable for contributory and vicarious liability. The technology in P2P and file sharing has evolved since Napster. Decentralized and hybrid models have replaced centralized technologies such as Napster.

P2P file sharing itself is not illegal. This technology can be used for legal purposes because it is capable of substantial non infringing uses according to the Sony doctrine. Nevertheless, the majority of P2P users distribute copyrighted materials without authorization from the copyright holders. In *Metro-Goldwyn-Mayer Studios, Inc v. Grokster*, the Ninth Circuit affirmed the applicability of the Sony doctrine to P2P file sharing. In this case, the court determined that P2P software distributors *Grokster* and *StreamCast Networks* could not be found liable as contributory infringers because, like Sony doctrine, their products were capable of substantial non infringing uses. On appeal to the Supreme Court, the Ninth Circuit decision was vacated and remanded with the Court taking a very dim view of Grokster's affirmative actions in promoting the infringing activity.

Even though users have the primary liability in these cases, the ISP could be found indirectly liable. Most of the litigation regarding vicarious liability against Internet intermediaries is related to actions against developers of P2P software. Contributory infringement has also been considered by courts in P2P cases. In Napster case, the ISP was found guilty for contributory infringement. The court determined that Napster had materially contributed to the infringement by providing the support services that allowed users to find and download music.

6   Cloud Computing Service Providers Liability for Copyright Infringement

The safe harbor and fair use principles have also been used by courts in the USA to deal with copyright infringement regarding cloud computing service providers' liability.

The first case related to cloud computing service providers' liability for copyright infringement in this country is *Capitol Records, Inc. v. MP3tunes, LLC*, also known as "MP3tunes case". In this case, the court discusses if cloud computing service providers are eligible for protection under the safe harbors created by DMCA.

EMI Inc. and fourteen record companies and music publishers claimed copyright infringement against MP3tunes, a cloud-storage that allows its users to store music in an online locker. MP3tunes offered a hybrid private-public cloud service in MP3tunes.com, and also owns Sideload.com as a second website. Sideload.com is a search engine site that allows users to search links on the Internet to download (or "sideload") music, and upload it to an MP3tunes digital locker. Once a song is added to an online locker, it can be downloaded from any user's device, and users can share and use copyrighted material without author's consent.

MP3tunes registered an agent with the Copyright Office to receive notices from alleged infringement from copyright owners and displayed the contact information of this agent in both sites. MP3 tunes received a takedown notice from EMI, identifying 350 song titles and links indexed in Sideload.com that connected the users to sites infringing EMI's copyrights. MP3tunes removed the links identified by EMI, and terminated the accounts of repeat infringers who violated copyrights by sharing the content of their lockers with other users, but did not remove copies of those songs from its users' lockers.

EMI claimed secondary liability for copyright infringement against MP3tunes for providing the means that allows end-users to violate EMI's copyrights, and argued that MP3tunes is ineligible for protection under DMCA because it failed to reasonably implement a repeat infringer policy by not identifying users who had sideloaded works identified in the takedown notices, and failed to act to remove songs from users' lockers that were sideloaded from websites identified in the notices.

The court found MP3tunes was eligible for the DMCA protections, and addressed a significant issue emerging in the cloud regarding EMI's claims [5]. The court ruled that MP3tunes had the duty not only to delete links to infringing materials publicly displayed on Sideload.com, but also the duty to remove songs stored in users' personal lockers which were downloaded from such links.

Regarding users' activity, the court distinguishes between blatant infringers, who know they lack authorization, and users who download content for their personal entertainment, and do not know for certain if the material they are downloading violates the copyrights of others. Blatant infringers are those who upload content and allow others to experience or copy the work. In this case, MP3tunes terminated the accounts of repeat infringers who violated copyrights by sharing the content of their lockers with other users. Fair use doctrine may protect a user who copies a song from his/her hard drive into cloud, but fair use will not excuse a user who uses a cloud service to share copyrighted material [2].

Even though the court determined the cloud service provider was entitled to safe harbors in this case, some problems can arise regarding this matter when the cloud services are private. The problem with this kind of cloud services is the difficulty for copyright holders to detect copyright infringement, and the ineffectiveness of takedown notices. Because of their private nature, it is almost impossible for copyright holders to detect an infringement in private cloud services, and providers may rarely receive takedown notices. The decision on MP3tunes does not extend to a private cloud service unaccompanied by a service like Sideload because takedown notices have little effect on private cloud services [2]. This kind of notices have little effect on private cloud services because the use of these services is private.

7   Conclusions

Safe harbor provisions and fair use are essential doctrines in copyright law. The DMCA establishes the safe harbor defense rules as a limitation of liability for ISPs regarding copyright infringement by Internet users.

The third safe harbor is applicable to cloud computing services. To be eligible for safe harbor provisions, cloud computing services provider must meet the statutory requirements for the DMCA's safe harbor, and must implement an effective takedown notice policy. If the service provider qualifies for safe harbor protection under the DMCA, the service provider is immune from damages caused by users.

Users can access and use copyrighted material without author's consent under fair use principles. Fair use doctrines may protect a user who copies a song from his/her hard drive into cloud, but fair use will not excuse a user who uses a cloud service to share copyrighted material.

Regarding the adequacy of current law to resolve copyright issues arising from cloud computing, it is noticed that in the MP3tunes case, the court determined that the cloud computing service provider was eligible for DMCA protection because the service provider met the statutory requirements for the DMCA's safe harbor and implemented an effective takedown notice policy. Even though the court determined that the DMCA's safe harbor principles were applicable to cloud computing services providers, the nature of certain services, like private clouds, represents a new challenge in copyright legal protection in this field.

References

1. Mell, P., Grance, T.: The NIST Definition of Cloud computing. Recommendations of the National Institute of Standards and Technology. Special Publication 800-145 (2011), http://csrc.nist.gov/publications/nistpubs/800-145/SP800-145.pdf
2. Leary, B.: Safe Harbor Startups: Liability Rulemaking under the DMCA. New York University Law Review 87, 1135–1171 (2012)
3. Ficsor, M.J.: The WIPO "Internet Treaties" and Copyright in the "Cloud". In: ALAI Congress (2012), http://www.alai.jp/ALAI2012/program/paper/The%20WIPO%20Internet%20Treaties%20and%20copyright%20in%20the%20Cloud%20%EF%BC%88Dr.%20Mih%C3%A1ly%20J.%20Ficsor%EF%BC%89.pdf
4. Seng, D.: Comparative Analysis of the National Approaches to the Liability of Internet Intermediaries, http://www.wipo.int/export/sites/www/copyright/en/doc/liability_of_internet_intermediaries.pdf
5. Bensalem, D.: Comparative Analysis of Copyright Enforcement in the Cloud under U.S. and Canadian Law: The Liability of Internet Intermediaries. Master thesis, University of Toronto (2012), https://tspace.library.utoronto.ca/bitstream/1807/33922/3/Bensalem_David_201211_LLM_thesis.pdf

Clouding Big Data: Information Privacy Considerations

John N. Gathegi

School of Information, University of South Florida
4202 E. Fowler Ave., Tampa, FL 33620, USA
jgathegi@usf.edu

Abstract. Advances in data storage and mining technologies have brought increasing attention to cloud computing and Big Data. One of the foci of this attention has been in the areas of privacy. The ubiquitous collection and analysis of data that enable predictions about human behavior and states is threatening our traditional notion of privacy, and bringing into question the notion of anonymity by aggregating data. This paper argues that a legalistic approach might not be sufficient to address the emerging privacy issues, and that we might consider looking at ethics as an additional avenue to arrive at some solutions.

Keywords: Big data, privacy, legal aspects, cloud computing, ethics.

1 Introduction

Much has been written recently about Big Data. What is apparent in most of this discussion is the lack of a precise definition of what the phrase means. We should therefore begin this chapter by adopting and modifying one of the many meanings of Big Data that exists among diverse scholars in the field. A good place to start is by describing characteristics of Big Data.

Most definitions of Big Data will include words relating to the collection from a variety of sources a huge amount of data that is often seemingly unrelated and aggregating this data in vast depository systems using highly complex database management software. Rubinstein [1] offers three defining characteristics of Big Data: (a) the "availability of massive data" that is continuously being collected, (b) utilization of fast computing, high data-rate transfer systems with massive storage systems that utilize the cloud computing model, and (c) new complex techniques for storing and analyzing such volume of data.

When one examines these characteristics, it seems like we are describing a well-known cycle that has been observed in the development of information technology: more data, faster computers, and novel analytic techniques. What distinguishes Big Data therefore, is the sheer scope of the data that can be stored, the utilization of the cloud model for this storage and more importantly, the sophistication of the techniques for mining this data.

1.1 Data Collection

As Rubinstein [1] and others have rightly observed, the amount of data being collected is increasing by orders of magnitude. Data is constantly collected through

J.N. Gathegi et al. (Eds.): IMCW 2013, CCIS 423, pp. 64–69, 2014.

various means: for example, online, through mobile devices, location tracking systems, and data sharing applications. Think of Google: user data is collected from email data (gmail), search data (google search engine), web navigation data, geographic location (google maps), voice and video communication data (gmail), image management and processing data, foreign language interest data (translate google), and more. The sobering fact is that there are many "google-like" applications out there.

Then there is the web 2.0 user generated data from popular social networking sites that includes personal data that is incredibly voluntarily shared among users. Think of Facebook, for example: there are almost one billion users uploading and sharing personal information. Terry predicts that much of data contributing to Big Data will be what he terms 'exhaust data' "created unintentionally as a byproduct of social networks, web searches, smartphones, and other online behaviors" [2].

To top it all, we are increasingly seeing smart environment interactions and monitoring as more and more devices get connected with each other through online communication, in the world of the so-called Internet of Things. In fact, some scholars predict that it is from the Internet of Things that Big Data will increasingly be derived [2].

1.2   Data Mining

Data mining refers to the extraction of information from the mass of data contained in Big Data. What is special about data mining is that the use of sophisticated statistical methods complex algorithms leads to the emergence of new patterns not previously discernible. These patterns may lead to the development of new associations, new meanings, and new knowledge [1].

It is therefore not too difficult to imagine the kind of treasure trove that is available to social media networks and search engine companies such as Google. For instance, Google has at its disposal personal data in the form of email, voice and video data from its gmail service, search data from its search engine, translation data from its translation service, geographic locational data from its maps service, among others. Facebook has about a billion users uploading personal information on a daily basis.

While there are major benefits of data mining to industry and society, for example in the areas of health and traffic management, there are downsides as well, in the form of threats to individual privacy [3]. Rubinstein [1] has noted several intertwined trends that he says pose serious challenges to privacy. He points to the proliferation of social networking sites, developments in cloud computing, ubiquity of mobile devices physical sensors and advances in data mining technologies. These trends encourage the sharing of personal data by individuals, the transmission of geo-locational data, and the aggregation and analysis of data sourced from a variety of sources. Terry [2] reminds us that data aggregation and customer profiling is not a new phenomenon. What is remarkable about Big Data now is the scale at which data is collected, and the developing sophistication of predictive analytics.

1.3   De-identification, Aggregation, and Re-identification

One of the advantages of data aggregation is that data can be analyzed at a level where individual identification is not necessary. In fact, most data is de-identified before it is aggregated, thus providing a measure of anonymity and privacy for individuals. However, increasingly sophisticated methods have evolved that allow for re-identification of de-identified data subjects, using non-personal data obtained from mining aggregated data [4].

2   Privacy Issues

Re-identification of data subjects directly threatens privacy by discarding the meaning of anonymity in aggregated data. It eviscerates the right to be forgotten, if ever there was such a right. Individual subject data is very valuable in the marketplace as can be demonstrated by Walmart's purchase of the Facebook application Social Calendar in 2012, even though it already owned ShopyCat, another Facebook application, clearly demonstrating that it could build its own applications. Obviously what interested Walmart was not the Social Calendar itself, but the individualized data that came with it, including 110 million birthdays/events and 400,000 monthly user usage data [5].

It is clear that de-identification is very frequently reversible. Tene and Polonetsky [4] note that dealing with the problem of re-identification comes down to balancing privacy on the one hand, and social benefit on the other. To illustrate this, they pose a problem where an analysis of de-identified search engine logs, where there is a "z" chance of re-identification of a subset of users, facilitates the identification of an "x" percentage of cases that are life-threatening and leads to saving "y" lives. The question they ask is whether society should permit this type of analysis.

There are many examples of cases where data that was supposed to be anonymous was released to the public, where researchers were then able to de-anonymize the data. One such example involved researchers at Harvard University who were studying changes in Facebook users' friendships and interests over time. They released the data they had collected because it was thought to be anonymous, but other researchers were able to de-anonymize some parts of the database [4].

But some cases have involved going from aggregated data and using analytical results to compare with known individualized data. This happened with a group of researchers at Stanford University whose analysis of data from adverse effect reporting data sets enabled them to create a "symptomatic footprint" for drugs that induced diabetes. Through the analysis, they discovered that the simultaneous use of an anti-depressant drug and a cholesterol-reducing drug resulted in diabetic-level increases in blood glucose. Using the footprint, they identified two pairs of drugs with this particular effect. They then analyzed search engine logs from Bing to see if people who searched for both drugs were also more likely to report diabetic symptoms than those who only searched for one of the drugs. The data supported their hypothesis of the interaction, and this helped save about a million lives [4].

2.1   Predictive Analytics

Increasingly sophisticated analytical tools have spawned the field of predictive analytics, where predictions about phenomena can be made from an analysis of data mined from Big Data. But there are serious concerns with this predictive ability. This has already been demonstrated in real life by the Target company case, where the company collected data on the purchase patterns of woman customers and were able, from an analysis of that data, to identify pregnancies and predict due dates. This led the company in one instance sending pre-natal and post-natal material to a young woman whose father became very upset as he had no idea the daughter was pregnant. Similarly, MIT researchers were in 2009 able to design a program that would analyze Facebook friendships and was thus able to predict male sexual orientation [6].

But the predictive analysis can raise issues even at the societal level. For instance, there are concerns that it could lead to the creation of police "pre-crime" departments that arrest individuals from decisions made on the basis of predictions of committing a future crime. Also, predictions could lead to redlining neighborhoods in insurance or social services coverage. As Tene and Polonetsky [4] point out:

> In a big data World, what calls for scrutiny is often not the accuracy of the raw data but rather the accuracy of the inferences drawn from the data. Inaccurate, manipulative or discriminatory conclusions may be drawn from perfectly innocuous, accurate data.

Concomitant with the predictive analytics problem is the automated decision-making that data mining system often make about individuals, regarding such things as their creditworthiness and insurance eligibility. These decisions are often made without any human intervention and there is little opportunity for the individuals to give their feedback or question the underlying data. Even if they wanted to give notice to the individuals concerned before using their data, Big Data miners cannot know in advance what they will find and thus cannot give notice of purpose for the information and the use to which it will be put. Relying on informed consent is likewise impossible, because data subjects cannot be able to monitor all the correlations and new patterns that will be produced by mining their data [2].

3   Big Data and Society

Industry is not the only Big Data driver. President Obama launched a significant Big Data research and development initiative in 2012 to bolster the study of the extraction of information from large heterogeneous data sets. Thus, with industry, social behavior, and government behind it, Big Data will only grow larger and the privacy problems associated with it are going to grow not in tandem, but exponentially.

Big Data has however also exposed deep inequalities in the power balance between the data generators and the data holders. Manovich [7] states that there are three classes of people in the Big Data world: the ones creating data either deliberately or by leaving digital footprints, those with the ability to collect the data, and the few privileged ones who have data analytical expertise. He sees these groups as forming a pyramid, with the data generators at the base, and the experts at the apex.

Tene and Polonetsky [4] note that presently the benefits of Big Data do not accrue to individuals whose data is harvested, only to big businesses that use such data:

> those who aggregate and mine this data neither view their information assets as public goods held on trust nor seem particularly interested in protecting the privacy of their data subjects. The truth lies in the opposite because the big data business model is selling information about their data subjects.

To make Big Data less of a pyramid, Tene and Polonetsky [4] advocate empowering individuals to control their personal information by giving them "meaningful rights to access their data in usable, machine-readable format." They cite two major advantages of doing this: first, giving this kind of power to individuals would unleash "innovation for user-side applications and services; second, it would provide users an incentive to participate in the data economy "by aligning their own self-interest with broader societal goals" [4].

4   Big Data Research Ethics

It is unlikely that we are going to find the answers to the privacy and security issues in Big Data and the cloud by simply relying on law and regulations. It might be time to go beyond the law and look into the ethics of Big Data research. For example, does the mere availability of the data make research ethical? The Target, Harvard, and Stanford examples we gave earlier underline the importance of this question.

The problem is compounded by the fact that "research ethics boards have insufficient understanding of the process of anonymizing and mining data, or the errors that can lead to data becoming personally identifiable," as well as the fact that the effects of such errors "may not be realized until many years into the future" [2].

Terry also notes that at the data generation stage, data contributors, such as social networkers, usually do not have researchers as their audience. Furthermore, "many have no idea of the processes currently gathering and using their data" [2]. As he further notes, there is a difference between being in public and being public. Ohm [3] cautions us that while many benefits of Big Data mining have been touted, we should be ready to interrogate the balance between these benefits and the attendant privacy risks.

5   Conclusion

Observations of trends so far point to the conclusion that Big Data is here to stay. It is also evident that Big Data management and exploitation is increasing happening in the cloud environment. What has not been so apparent is that this combination of Big Data and the cloud environment is gradually erasing the notion of public/private distinction. Looking solely at legal solutions might not provide guidance on how to tackle the increasingly complex privacy issues that are unlikely to diminish in their frequency of occurrence.

References

1. Rubinstein, I.: Big Data: The End of Privacy or a New Beginning? International Data Privacy Law (2013), http://ssrn.com/abstract=2157659
2. Terry, N.: Protecting Patient Privacy in the Age of Big Data. University of Missouri-Kansas City Law Review 81(2), 385–415 (2012)
3. Ohm, P.: The Underwhelming Benefits of Big Data. University of Pennsylvania Law Review 161, 339–346 (2013)
4. Tene, O., Polonetsky, J.: Big Data for All: Privacy and User Control in the Age of Analytics (2013), http://ssrn.com/abstract=2149364
5. Ness, D.: Information Overload: Why the Omnipresent Technology and the Rise of Big Data Shouldn't Spell the End for Privacy as We Know It. Cardozo Arts and Entertainment Law Journal 31, 925–955 (2013)
6. Jernigan, C., Mistree, B.: Gaydar: Facebook Friendships Expose Sexual Orientation. First Monday 14, 10 (2009), http://firstmonday.org/ojs/index.php/fm/article/view/2611/2302
7. Manovich, L.: Trending: The Promises and the Challenges of Big Social Data (2011), http://www.manovich.net/DOCS/Manovich_trending_paper.pdf

The Influence of Recent Court Cases Relating to Copyright Changes in Cloud Computing Services in Japan

Takashi Nagatsuka

Department of Library, Archival and Information Studies, Tsurumi University, Tsurumi
2-1-3,Tsurumi-ku,Yokohama, 230-8501, Japan
nagatsuka-t@tsurumi-u.ac.jp

Abstract. The utilization of cloud computing is still inadequate and the cloud computing services are believed; to have a huge potential for development in the future in Japan. Here, the scope of the cloud computing services is limited to offer individual users the opportunity of storing copyrighted works on an online platform. The cloud computing services include online platforms for publishing photographs and videos, social networking sites and digital locker services. In Japan, meanwhile, the legality of digital locker services centers mainly on whether a service provider falls within the definition of a principal committing copyright infringement, because there is no general fair use exception in Japanese copyright law. In 2011, the Japanese Supreme Court reversed the decision of a lower court which found no infringement based on the right of making broadcasts transmittable or the right of public transmission. This paper examines the influence of recent court cases relating to the copyright within the scope of changes brought about by cloud computing in Japan.

Keywords: Cloud computing, cloud computing services, digital locker services, copyrighted works, Japanese copyright law.

1 Introduction

While cloud computing services are being utilized throughout most developed countries, such services are still in their infancy in Japan. The expectations, however, are high. [1]. The NIST describes cloud computing as follows: "Cloud computing is a model for enabling ubiquitous, convenient, on-demand network access to a shared pool of configurable computing resources that can be rapidly provisioned and released with minimal management effort or service provider interaction" [2]. Yet, cloud computing is still an evolving paradigm.

Cloud computing services include online platforms for publishing photographs and videos, social networking sites and digital locker services [3], as well as all manner of digital document storage and diffusion. Cloud computing services provide storage facilities and data flows among servers potentially located beyond what are thought of as traditional national borders. This raises legal questions concerning the definable location of the data in regard to access, use, copyright and protection of the data.

J.N. Gathegi et al. (Eds.): IMCW 2013, CCIS 423, pp. 70–79, 2014.

In Japan, meanwhile, the legality of digital locker services such as Rokuraku- II [4], the Rokuga Net [5], MYUTA [6], TV Break (formerly, "Pandora TV") [7] and Maneki TV [8], centers mainly on whether the actions of a service provider have infringed the copyright law, because there is no general fair use exception in Japanese copyright law [9]. In 2011, the Japanese Supreme Court reversed the decision of a lower court which found no infringement based on the right of making broadcasts transmittable or the right of public transmission, in both cases of Rokuraku- II [10] and Maneki TV [11].

Meanwhile, Japanese Copyright Law was amended in 2012 to provide punitive sanctions for downloading copyrighted works that have been uploaded illegally, even when this is done for private use [12].

This paper examines the influence of recent court cases relating to the cloud computing services on the copyright scope changes in Japan.

2   The Cloud Computing Services in Japan

If the example of digital social media services such as *Facebook*, *MySpace* and *Twitter* is anything to go by, Japan is somewhat slow to adapt to imported technology. In great contrast to practices overseas, Japanese companies are still cold to the idea of using such social media as part of their day to day operations [13]. The Japan Business Federation (Keidanren), the nation's largest business lobby, held a meeting in March 2012 for the purpose of discussing policy issues related to cloud computing. The report of that meeting stated that "cloud computing enables resource-shorted entrepreneurs, small businesses and developing countries to access information and to build communication technology (ICT) infrastructure at low cost and as needed. As a result, the benefits of cloud computing are not limited to just the ICT sector, the 'cloud' is an important platform for the growth of all industries" [1].

In July 2012, the Japanese government announced a new strategy for "Japanese Renewal". The statement mentioned that expectations are high in Japan regarding the benefits to come from cloud computing because sharing of information is critical for Japan [14]. Moreover, cloud computing services are already changing the style of business and public services in Japan, and huge development is expected particularly in the service industry. In order to further develop cloud computing services in Japan, the Intellectual Property Strategic Program (IPSP) report states that legal risks must be addressed and environmental improvement around cloud computing services must be promoted [15]. As pointed out in the report, new information terminals are becoming more widely used along with the development of cloud computing services. The delay and loss in viewing videos across national borders and via mobile communication are caused by the presence of legal risks: the threat of legal action often results in hindrance in the dissemination of digital matter, be it videos, audio or text.

The investment effects of the Cartoon Network, et al. v. Cablevision decision in the U.S. and court rulings in France and Germany on venture capital (VC) investment in U.S. cloud computing firms relative to the EU were analyzed by Borek et al. [16].

Then, the effects of the French and German court rulings on VC investment on cloud computing firms in these countries were separately analyzed. The results of those analyses suggest that decisions around the scope of copyrights can have economically and statistically significant impacts on investment and innovation.

3   The Cloud Computing Services and Limitations on the Reproduction for Private Use

The Japanese Copyright Act has explicitly enumerated limitation provisions depending on the kind of bundle rights and relevant exploitations. One such limitation is the private use limitation for the reproduction right,

> Article 30 (Reproduction for private use): (1) Except in the cases listed below, it shall be permissible for the user of a work that is the subject of a copyright (below in this Subsection simply referred to as a "work") to reproduce the work for his personal use or family use or other equivalent uses within a limited scope (hereinafter referred to as "private use"): … [12].

Customers of certain cloud services may wonder whether they are liable for infringement of reproduction rights concerning the use which falls within a "private use". Even if each customer is exempted from liability based on such a limitation, a service provider may nonetheless still be liable for the customer's exploitation of the particular copyrighted works under what is known as the "Karaoke theory" or a variation thereof [17].

3.1   The Karaoke Theory

The "Karaoke theory" is now prevalent among copyright infringement cases in Japan. The Karaoke theory was originally adopted to decide whether a manager of a traditional Japanese Karaoke bar was liable for infringement of the "right of performance" on copyrighted musical works when it provided occasions for its customers to perform such works. Article 22 of the Copyright Act states that the author shall have the exclusive right to perform his work publicly ("publicly" means for the purpose of making a work seen or heard directly by the public) [12]. Copyright holders want to charge the manager of such a Karaoke bar instead of an individual customer [17]. Beyond the Karaoke bar case, the Karaoke theory has been more broadly applied to other kinds of services when the provider is merely an indirect practitioner, but the customers directly exploit particular copyrighted works (the so-called "variation" of the Karaoke theory). When the Karaoke theory is applied to the cloud computing services, careful consideration is needed to determine whether or not the reproduction of copyrighted material provided falls within the description of "private use".

3.2   Cloud Computing Services and Copyrighted Works

In this paper, the scope of the cloud computing services is limited to offering individual users the opportunity of storing copyrighted works on an online platform. This definition still includes various types of online platforms and services. The first type of cloud computing services deals with primarily visual/audio material: online platforms for posting photographs such as *Flickr, Photozou* and *Picasa*, or online platforms for posting videos such as *YouTube* and *niconico*, allowing individual users to create content and make it available on the Internet (Fig. 1).

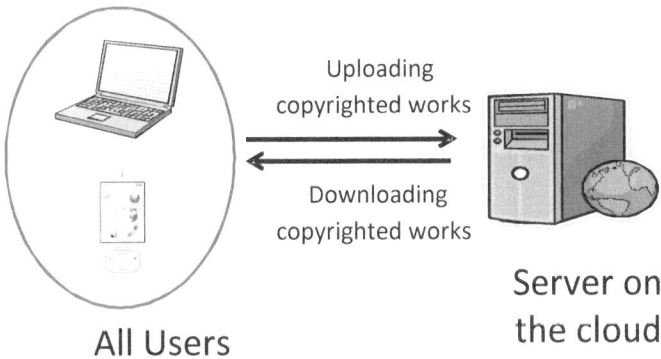

Fig. 1. Online platform for posting photographs or videos

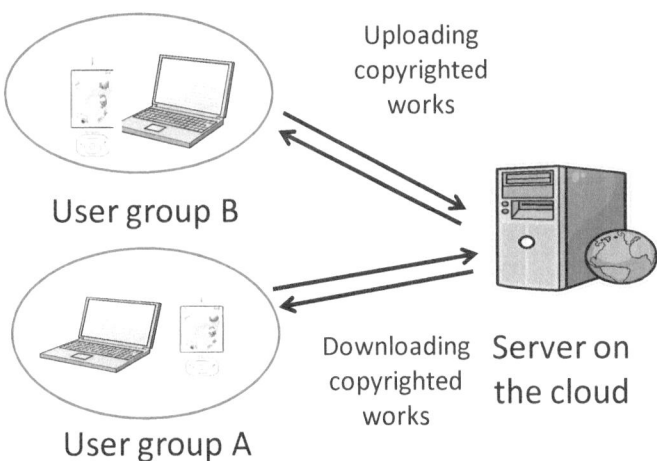

Fig. 2. SNS service as online platform allowing individual users to post various types of works, such as texts, photographs and videos

The second type of cloud computing services concerns social networking sites such as *Facebook, Line* and *Twitter*, which allow individual users to post various types of works such as texts, messaging, photographs and videos (Fig. 2). In this case, the target audience is a specific group of Internet users having access to the personal webpages of the individual user providing content. In a similar case, the data of copyrighted works are uploaded to a server located within a particular organization, then access to and sharing of data is granted to members of that organization (Fig. 3).

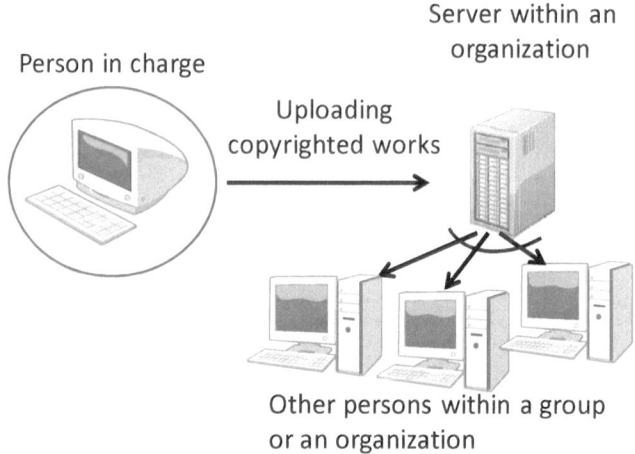

Fig. 3. Uploading the data of copyrighted works to a server within an organization and browsing it in the same or other place

The third type of cloud computing services is a digital locker service, which allows individual users to upload personal copies of protected works to their own personal cloud storage space for later downloading or streaming on multiple devices, or via a private video recorder allowing users to obtain recordings of TV programs for the purpose of watching them at a more convenient time or place (Fig. 4). In this case, the target audience is confined to the individual user [3].

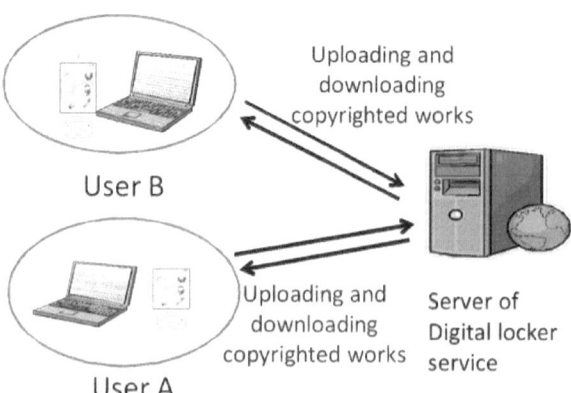

Fig. 4. Digital locker service allowing individual users to upload personal copies of protected works to personal cloud storage space

3.3   Court Decisions Regarding the Cloud Computing Services

Table 1 displays information on some court cases relating to cloud computing services in Japan. The legality of personal locker or "placeshifting" services as a type of cloud computing services centers mainly on whether a service provider falls within the definition of a principal committing copyright infringement. In Japan, indirect infringement of copyright does not only entitle copyright owners to injunctive remedies, but also to monetary remedies of damages. Most courts have applied an overall consideration standard such as the Karaoke theory or its variation to this issue. Because courts apply an overall consideration standard, it is therefore difficult to find the critical factor that would make a personal locker or "placeshifting" service legal or illegal.

Table 1. Court cases relating to the cloud computing services in Japan

Date	Case	Court
Nov. 15, 2005	Rokuga Net	INTELL. HIGH Ct.
May 25, 2007	MYUTA	Tokyo D. Ct.
Sep. 8, 2010	TV Break (formerly, "Pandora TV)	INTELL. HIGH Ct.
Jan. 31, 2012	Maneki TV	INTELL. HIGH Ct.
Jan. 31, 2012	Rokuraku-II	INTELL. HIGH Ct.

3.4   The Rokuga Net

The Rokuga Net was a service that enabled its customers who lived abroad to view Japanese television programs. The provider placed a personal computer together with television tuner having the function of receiving and recording television programs at the disposal of each user. Each user operated his or her own TV-personal computer from home through the Internet to reserve recordings of programs and transmitted the recorded files from his or her own personal computer to the provider's server and then downloaded the transmitted files to his or her own TV-personal computer from anywhere. The Intellectual Property High Court, taking into consideration the actions of copying television programs as a whole, concluded that the Rokuga Net service was the principal committing infringement of the "reproduction right" [5].

3.5   MYUTA

MYUTA was a service that enabled its customers to connect to the Internet from a personal computer and a mobile phone. The service allowed a user to upload music recorded on their own computer such as from their CDs and store it on the provider's servers under his or her own personal and restricted account, and then to download music to his or her mobile phone for listening. The music could only be downloaded to the user's mobile phone and was not available publicly or to any other users. The provider claimed that essentially the parties that copy/send the music are the users themselves and that they do not send the music to unspecified parties in order not to violate any copyright laws. The Tokyo District Court concluded that the central servers in the MYUTA system are owned and managed by the provider, and that the provider is guilty of copyright infringement unless it obtained consent from the copyright holder [6].

3.6   TV Break (Formerly, "Pandora TV")

TV Break was a service that allowed its customers to post and share videos on its website. The service allowed a user to upload video recorded on his or her own computer, and the user stored it on the provider's servers and then other users downloaded the video to their own computer. The Intellectual Property High Court concluded that the service of TV Break was the principal committing infringement of the "reproduction right" and "right of public transmission" by storing videos from users on the provider's servers and distributing them to other users [7].

3.7   Maneki TV

Maneki TV was a service that enabled its customers who lived abroad to view Japanese television programs. The service used a device called a "Base Station" that converted television broadcasts into digital data and transmitted them to a customer's personal viewing device through an individual customer's remote control. The Tokyo District Court and Intellectual Property High Court concluded that the service of Maneki TV did not principally commit the infringement of the "right to make his performance transmittable" and "right of public transmission" by transmitting television programs to a customer's personal viewing device through an individual customer's remote control [18].

3.8   Rokuraku-II

Rokuraku-II was a service that enabled its customers who lived abroad to view Japanese television programs. The service used two devices called "Parent Device Rokuraku" that converted television broadcasts into digital data and transmitted them to a customer's personal viewing device through an individual customer's remote control, and "Child Device Rokuraku" that was set in each customer's home. The Tokyo District Court approved the plaintiffs' allegation, and the Intellectual Property High Court concluded that the service of Rokuraku-II was the principal committing infringement of the "reproduction right" by transmitting television programs to a customer's personal viewing device through an individual customer's remote control [5]. However, the Supreme Court judged the defendant was a direct infringer of the reproduction rights [10]. This court case seems similar to the recent court case of Maneki TV, but the outcomes are different [11].

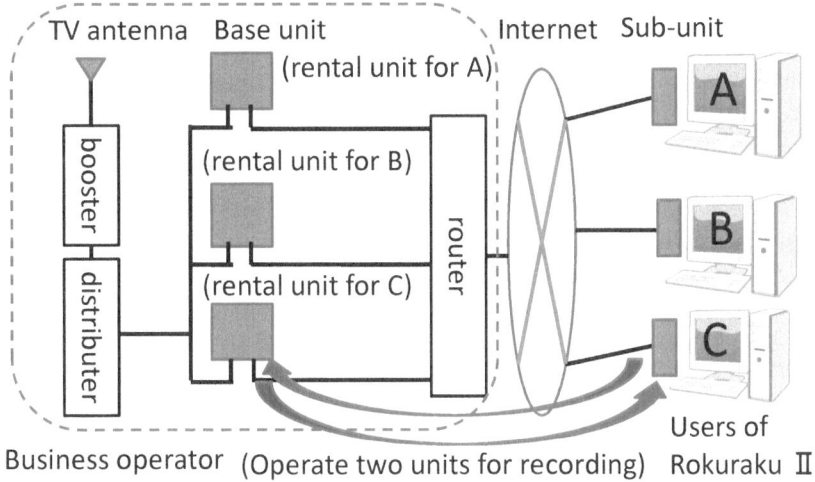

Fig. 5. The conceptual diagram of Rokuraku-II as a cloud computing service

4   Conclusions

Most courts in Japan have applied the Karaoke theory or its variation to the cases relating to cloud computing services. Copyright holders want to charge the manager of such a Karaoke bar instead of an individual customer [17]. Beyond the Karaoke bar case, the Karaoke theory has been more broadly applied to other kinds of services when the provider is merely an indirect conduit, but the customers directly exploit particular copyrighted works; the so-called "variation" of the Karaoke theory, which was applied to personal locker or "placeshifting" services as a type of cloud computing services[10], [11].

The legality of personal locker or "placeshifting" services as a type of cloud computing services, centers mainly on whether a service provider falls within the definition of a principal committing copyright infringement, because there is no general fair use exception in Japanese copyright law [9]. As described earlier, the Japanese Supreme Court reversed the decisions of the lower court which found no infringement based on the right of making broadcasts transmittable or the right of public transmission in 2011 [10], [11]. Even if a user has the final option to reproduce or transmit a work, the person who enabled the reproduction or transmission other than the final option controls the outcome and should be considered to be the subject of the reproduction or transmission [19]. As affairs now stand, it is difficult to find the critical factor that would make a personal locker or "placeshifting" service legal or illegal. At present in Japan, there is no way to anticipate with any accuracy precisely what critical factors consistently lead to a service being deemed legal or illegal.

Moreover, cloud computing services are changing the style of business and public services, and are considered a service industry where huge development is expected. In order to develop a cloud computing service in Japan, the IPSP report states that legal risks must be resolved and environmental improvement must be promoted [15].

As pointed out in the report, while new information terminals are becoming more widely used along with the development of cloud computing services, the delay and loss in viewing videos cross national borders and via mobile communication are caused by the presence of legal risks.

The investment effects of the Cartoon Network, et al. v. Cablevision decision in the U.S. and court rulings in France and Germany were estimated from venture capital (VC) investment in U.S. cloud computing firms relative to the EU [16]. Findings suggest that decisions around the scope of copyrights can have economically and statistically significant impacts on investment and innovation.

With regard to improving the environment for cloud computing services in Japan, the use of common content is being promoted for multiple information terminals, such as smart phones and tablet terminals. It is important to consider how to resolve legal risks associated with clarifying the extent of private duplication and indirect infringement in the copyright system, and then to apply necessary measures.

Revisions in Japanese Copyright Law, make it illegal to download sound files (music, voice, ring-tones, etc.) or video files (movie films, television programs, etc.) that are uploaded in violation of copyright laws. Even if for personal use, downloading those files is prohibited [12]. Something is either legal or illegal. The revised Japanese Copyright Law became effective from October 1, 2012. This amendment of the law in 2012 which provides punitive sanctions for downloading copyrighted works that have been uploaded illegally, even when this is done for private use, will discourage individuals from using cloud computing services in Japan.

References

1. Keidanren, U.S.-Japan Cloud Computing Working Group Report (2012), `http://www.keidanren.or.jp/en/policy/2012/073_report.html`
2. Mell, P., Grance, T.: The NIST Definition of Cloud Computing - Recommendations of the National Institute of Standards and Technology. NIST Special Publication 800-145 (2011)
3. Senftleben, M.: Breathing Space for Cloud-Based Business Models - Exploring the Matrix of Copyright Limitations, Safe Harbours and Injunctions (2013), `http://dx.doi.org/10.2139/ssrn.2241259`
4. Rokuraku-II.: Intell. High Ct., Japan (2012), `http://www.courts.go.jp/hanrei/pdf/20120201164305.pdf`
5. Rokuga Net.: Intell. High Ct., Japan (2005), `http://www.courts.go.jp/hanrei/pdf/842BD42DCC4020FC492570C100253DFF.pdf`
6. MYUTA: Tokyo D. Ct., Japan (2007), `http://www.courts.go.jp/hanrei/pdf/20070528141551.pdf`
7. TV Break (formerly, "Pandora TV"): Intell. High Ct., Japan (2010), `http://www.courts.go.jp/hanrei/pdf/20100909131245.pdf`
8. Maneki TV: Intell. High Ct., Japan (2012), `http://www.courts.go.jp/hanrei/pdf/20120201162709.pdf`
9. Kidokoro, I.: Cloud Service Providers' Copyright Infringement Liability - Comparison of Case Laws between Japan and the U.S. The conference report of Information Network Law Association Japan (2012) (in Japanese)

10. Rokuraku-II.: Supreme Ct., Japan (2011), http://www.courts.go.jp/hanrei/pdf/20110120144645.pdf
11. Maneki TV: Supreme Ct., Japan (2011), http://www.courts.go.jp/hanrei/pdf/20110118164443.pdf
12. Japanese Law Translation Database System, http://www.japaneselawtranslation.go.jp/
13. Cruz, X.: The State of Cloud Computing Around the World: Japan. Cloud Times (2012), http://cloudtimes.org/2012/12/04/state-cloud-computing-around-world-japan/
14. National Policy Unit Cabinet Secretariat, Japan: Comprehensive Strategy for the Rebirth of Japan (2012), http://www.cas.go.jp/jp/seisaku/npu/pdf/20120731/20120731_en.pdf
15. Intellectual Property Strategy Headquarters, Prime Minister of Japan: Intellectual Property Strategic Program 2012 (2012), http://www.kantei.go.jp/jp/singi/titeki2/ipsp2012.pdf
16. Borek, C., Christensen, L.R., Hess, P., Lerner, J., Greg Rafert, G.: Lost in the Clouds: The Impact of Copyright Scope on Investment in Cloud Computing Ventures (2013), http://www.ccianet.org/index.asp?bid=11
17. Isoda, N.: Copyright Infringement Liability of Placeshifting Services in the United States and Japan. Washington Journal of Law, Technology & Artslaw, Technology & Arts Group Feature Article 7(2), 149–207 (2011)
18. Maneki TV: Intell. High Ct., Japan (2008), http://www.courts.go.jp/hanrei/pdf/20081216170214.pdf
19. Yamamoto, T.B.: Legal Liability for Indirect Infringement of Copyright in Japan. Comparative Law Yearbook of International Business 35, 1–20 (2013)

Government Participation in Digital Copyright Licensing in the Cloud Computing Environment

Jingzhu Wei and Shujin Cao

School of Information Management, Sun Yat-Sen University, No.132, East Outer Ring Rd,
510006 Guangzhou Higher Education Mega Center, China
{Weijzhu,Caosj}@mail.sysu.edu.cn

Abstract. Cloud computing represents a major development in the digital environment and is of great influence on the digital copyright system, breaking down the interests balancing mechanism between copyright creators, owners, distributors and users. Governments of many countries actively intervene in their copyright market. In the environment of cloud computing, how and to what extent government should participate in the digital copyright market as a part of commodities market deserves studying. This paper introduces some cases of Chinese government participation in digital copyright solutions with several projects (e.g., Copyright Cloud Project, and National Cultural Information Resources Sharing Project (NCIRSP)) and discusses the role and means of government participation in digital copyright licensing in the development of copyright markets. With respect to the cloud computing environment, this paper proposes how the government should take advantages of cloud computing technology to promote the diffusion and usage of digital resources, to make the market of digital copyright prosperous.

Keywords: Copyright, digital copyright licensing, government, cloud computing.

1   Introduction

1.1   Digital Copyright in China

The Copyright Law of China was published in 1990 "in accordance with the Constitution, for the purpose of protecting the copyright of authors in their literary, artistic and scientific works and rights and interests related to copyright, encouraging creation and dissemination of works", with the aim to encourage beneficial socialist spiritual civilization, the creation and dissemination of material civilization works to promote the development and prosperity of socialist culture and science [1, Article 1]. The fast development and popularity of digital technology has caused digital copyright problems in China and other countries all around the world. As a consequence, China amended the Copyright Act in 2001. The Copyright Act expressly provides for the

J.N. Gathegi et al. (Eds.): IMCW 2013, CCIS 423, pp. 80–91, 2014.
© Springer-Verlag Berlin Heidelberg 2014

protection of information network dissemination rights: the right of networks to disseminate information by providing wired or wireless work to the public so that members of the public can retrieve and work on it at the place and time of their choice [1, Article 10, Clause 12].This right is explained explicitly by the State Council through the enactment of the Regulation on Protection of the Right to Network Dissemination of Information. In 2010, the copyright law of China was amended for the second time. In March 2013, the third amendment of the copyright law begun and suggestions are now being collected from experts and the public [2].

The digital copyright market in China is developing at an unprecedented speed and scale. As for the network users in China, the number of network users has exceeded 564 million [3], and the number of users utilizing the Internet, mobile phone and handheld devices to read ranks first in the world [4]. As for online creation, the number of Internet writers having contracts with websites is more than one million [5]. What is more, there is an online writer who has been declared as holding the Guinness world record for having over 260 million readers and 100 months-worth of updates [3].

China's digital copyright market is maturing. To what extent government should participate in that market is an important issue. The relationship between government and market has been a much debated topic and it seems impossible to find a once and for all solution to the problem [6]. According to modern market economics theory, the combination of government intervention and market mechanism is the basic model of economic operation [7].

1.2   What Can Cloud Computing Change

China's copyright market development has made considerable progress. However, due to the lag in digital copyright legislation, imperfect industry mechanisms and other reasons, digital copyright licensing still has some drawbacks. These drawbacks are mainly caused by the delay in legislation [8], [9], lack of industry chain integration [10], and information asymmetry, among others. The unclear division of rights and obligations mainly attributed to the traditional copyright law cannot be extended to the Internet, as Jaeger et al. argued [11].

In 2006, Google's CEO Eric Schmidt put forward the concept of cloud computing for the first time at the Search Engine Strategies Conference. The main features of cloud computing include: shared, interactive and group intelligence; showing huge, high security and reliability; versatility; scalability; strong virtualization; low client requirements; and low cost [12].

Cloud computing has shown significant advantages for both users and businesses [13]. Users can use their own browser to backup the data they need to the cloud anytime, anywhere so as to not only solve the problems of local storage capacity insufficiency and data loss, but also restrict unauthorized sharing [14].

From the business management perspective, cloud computing provides a good approach to manage mass virtualization resources [15]. Editors can share files, information and applications wherever there is an Internet connection and can work on the same files [16]. More importantly, multi-terminal work cooperation and distribution can promote more coordination between the publishers, distributors and customers [17].

1.3   Digital Copyright Licensing in the Cloud Computing Environment

Cloud computing represents the turning point from individual service to centralized service in the network industry [18]. However, the development of the technology has not turned over the basic principle of copyright system: creation brings rights while usage needs permission [19].

As for digital copyright, cloud computing plays an important role in the integration of the digital copyright supply chain. Cloud computing service charges by rent rather than buy, so the cost can be reduced. Thus digital copyright industry chain in cloud can achieve capital flow integration, promoting implementation of digital copyright license and better profit distribution. How to take advantage of its benefits and avoid its deficiency and how to coordinate different interests of multiple copyright shareholders in the new environment have to be settled urgently.

2   Literature Review

2.1   Classical Theories of Government Participation in Economy

Classical theories in economics proposed different views on government's role in the market while they all affirmed the role of government in economy operation. Adam Smith is routinely caricatured as a champion of laissez-faire economic policies but he never made a blanket rejection of government. *The Wealth of Nations* is a treatise about economic development through good government [20]. Based on the elements of liberal economy, he proposed that the functions of government are detailing the work division, increasing capital and improving the capital usage [7]. According to Werhane [21], Smith did see many areas that are ripe for government regulation, as did Skinner [22], [8].

According to Goldsmith [8], Adam Smith highlighted three public rights - basic law and order, the right to property, and the enforcement of contracts [23]. These rights set the stage for increased bargaining and economic growth [24]. The legal fiction property is the bedrock for capitalism, since, obviously, people cannot give and get assets they do not 'own' [20]. In his *General Theory of Employment, Interest and Money*, Keynes [25] proposed the government function theory of state interventionism positing that free competitive market presumed in the liberalism theory did not exist in real life so market mechanism could not balance supply and demand independently [26].

2.2   Relationship between Government and Market

Follow the vein of free economy and government function study, Professor Zhao [27] viewed the function of government as economy regulation, market supervision, social administration and public service, which put the regulation and supervision of economy and market as the basis of government participation. He argues that free market without government participation would not exist and whether to participate in the market depends on whether the government can activate the market and promote the development of economy.

As for China, Steven N. Cheung further discusses government effect in the market economy from the angle of inter-country (government) competition and concluded that

Chinese economy's continuously rapid development resulted from interaction between government and market [28]. Li Ru [7] believes that both market mechanism and government participation have their strengths and weaknesses and need to play their roles respectively.

2.3   Government Participation in Copyright Market in China

Xuemin Zeng [29] suggested that China's copyright market has experienced three stages, leading to a stage of standardization and internationalization: From 1979 to 1990, Chinese government published related administrative regulations, organized several publishers to participate in international book fairs and exchange experiences of culture dissemination from abroad; From 1990 to 2000, copyright market was established during which time China published the copyright law and provisions relating to the implementation of international copyright conventions, and joined the Berne Convention and the Universal Copyright Convention. The development of copyright market has been under protection of law from that time. From 2000 till now, the copyright market in China is becoming standardized, large-scale, and international.

Jie Guo and Xiaoqiang Zhang [30] argue that the development of copyright trading of a country is related to the guidance and administration of its government. Chinese government should provide general policies of copyright trade, constructing platforms and improving information systems of copyright trade. Lanping Zhu [31] suggested that copyright protection mechanism is challenged in the environment of the Internet, which merits government intervention in order to protect the public interest.

2.4   Cloud Computing and Copyright

Technology development and copyright reform are always closely related. As a new technology, cloud computing has great influence on digital copyright [32]. From a global point of view, cloud computing will change the copyright system and affect copyright authorization [33]. The influence of cloud computing on digital copyright exists in five aspects: shaking traditional copyright theory and legislation construction, harder authorization, author's weaker position, lagging digital copyright market supervision and regulation, and judicial and law enforcement [34].

Cloud computing demands reflection on the gap between policy and technology. As Jaeger P. et al. pointed out, many of the problems at the nexus of policy and technology derive from trying to use print-based concepts of policy in an electronic world [35]. Cloud computing leads to changes in transaction costs [36]. It will upset the balance between copyright owners, users, and disseminators [34].

3   The Government is Active: Several Projects and Their Implications

The Chinese government has played a positive role in digital copyright market construction and contributed to digital copyright protection in a variety of ways.

3.1   Copyright Cloud (CC): Building Digital Copyright Supply Chain

Practice of Government Supported Copyright Cloud

Under the guidance of China Copyright Protection Center, the CC project co-sponsored by Beijing Oriental Yonghe International Copyright Trade Center was established in May 2012 [37]. The CC project is dedicated to digital copyright industry chain integration and management [38]. With a copyright credit certification system, the CC project has built a supply chain of digital copyright, and promoted a revenue-sharing mechanism [39]. Utilizing cloud computing technology, the project has built a copyright circulation environment and provides a p2p intelligent copyright supply chain [40].

Copyright supply chain has been regarded as an effective way for copyright market administration. However, how to complete a transaction is a problem in the new environment. It is expected that a self-service royalty checkout model will be integrated to solve the large number of authorization and propagation problems at the lowest cost, and government's coordination is still needed [41].

Theory of CC's Government Participation in the Hard and Soft Side

China Copyright Protection Center as a government agency, has led the creation of CC to integrate the digital industry chain and coordinate the benefit mechanism with cloud computing technology and promote the digital copyright protection and digital culture propagation. So this case can be seen as a mode of government participation in market supervision and management, fully taking advantages of cloud computing and playing its public service functions [27].

If we take the CC platform as the result of government participation, it belongs to the hard side of government participation. What is more, with the cloud computing platform, the government can further utilize its function of coordination and administration to achieve self-service royalty checkout model which can be considered as the government participation on the soft side.

3.2   National Cultural Information Resources Sharing Project (NCIRSP): The Statutory Licensing Notice System and Government Coordination

Practice of Government Coordination in NCIRSP

NCIRSP is a national construction project jointly organized and implemented by the Ministry of Culture and the Ministry of Finance since 2002. Its goal is to build an urban and rural public cultural service system network, making all kinds of information resources available throughout the country through this network coverage [42]. NCIRSP has integrated digital resources through modern information technologies, propagated resources through carriers such as Internet, satellite, television and mobile phones, and shared the resources relying on all branches of libraries, cultural centers and other public cultural facilities nationwide. For example, in rural areas, NCIRSP service system provides all kinds of rich cultural resources for grassroots residents through Internet or removable storage and CD-ROM, through indoor and outdoor concentrated slideshows, television and PC services, and others [43].

As for Copyright issues, NCIRSP adopts principles of "Copyright First[1]" and "Copyright one-vote veto[2]". In practice, channels to get copyright of digital resources include: reception, collection, procurement, agent processing, statutory licensing and so on [44]. As for film and other works invested by the state, the NCIRSP members could use them free of charge [45].

Theory of Government Participation in Public Welfare Service and Digital Licensing

A) Public Welfare Service. Government participation in public welfare service is definitely affirmed by contemporary administrative management and political economics theories [46]. As the guarantor of public interest, the government makes up the deficiency of market economy and increases the social benefits through its intervention and the economy is improved by its participation [47].

According to the "Information Network Transmission Right Protection Ordinance", resources meeting certain conditions are in within the scope of the statutory license conditions of China, which allows the provision of services via the Internet to help the poor [48]. Because NCIRSP is a public welfare project with a mandate of protecting information and cultural rights of people, it is within the scope of statutory license [49].

B) Digital Licensing. China Copyright Law 1990 provided four kinds of statutory license and Copyright Law 2010 added five more [1, Articles 23, 33, 40, 43-44]. Regulation on Protection of the Right to Network Dissemination of Information creates an announcement system for statutory license, which authorizes ICPs to provide works related to assisting the poor on planting and breeding, disease prevention and treatment, and disaster prevention and mitigation, and works meeting the fundamental cultural demands of the poor without licensing, but with remuneration to the copyright owners according to the announced standard [48]. The announcement system has been proposed by the Ministry of Culture in the second course of copyright law revision, which was eventually accepted by the legislature [50].

In 2005, the general office of the CPC forwarded a file on "Further Strengthening of the National Cultural Information Resources Sharing Project Construction Opinions", which affirmed that copyright works such as films invested by the state can be used freely by NCIRSP [51]. Ways of government purchases of public service mainly

---

[1]"Copyright first" refers to the pre-stage of cultural sharing project; the project team will organize consulting experts and carry out the negotiations with the copyright owners to get authorization to assure that every work used by the project is licensed.

[2]"Copyright one-vote veto" system is such that if there is one person among all stakeholders who does not give permission to use the work, then this work will not be included as an object in the NCIRSP.

include contract rent, public-private partnership, user charges and subsidies [52]. Digital copyright purchasing now is an important way for government to solve the copyright issues in the course of NCIRSP.

3.3   Government Buying for National Digital Library (NDL)

Practice of Government Buying for NDL
The National Digital Library Corp. Ltd. is a high-tech enterprise which belongs to the National Library of China and serving phase II of the National Library Project, namely the National Digital Library Project [53].

Relying on special resource and rich collection of China National Library, with the organization of information across the country and service network, NDL is the largest digital library in China. It has digital resources both from the museum's own digital resources, as well as those it obtains from the native digital resources.

Theory of Government buying for NDL
The core of public expenditure management is rational distribution and effective utilization of public resources and is an effective way of modern government budget implementation management [54]. NDL as the information provider and culture center of China is responsible for providing information nationwide. Purchase of digital copyright is a way to solve this problem.

However, as Wengeng Wang [54] pointed out, the institutional building of the government procurement system is mainly from the point of view of regulating procedures of government procurement, promoting fair competition among enterprises, as well as boosting the combat of corruption and building a clean government. Producing policy functions of government procurement have been considered, but the specific conditions of how to implement that is lacking, thus weakening the government's regulation and control.

From the above three cases, we can see that the Chinese government's participation in digital copyright licensing is the backbone of the development and prosperity of China's digital copyright market. At the same time, cultural industry has been merged into national strategic industry. The overall goal is to solve various problems of digital copyright with integration of government intervention and market mechanism during the procedure of digital copyright market formation and to combine that with the reform of the cultural system so as to promote the development of cultural industry at the national strategic level.

4   Government Participation in New Technology Environment: Two Levels

4.1   Government Intervention is always Needed

The copyright history told us that the balance mechanism of interests will be broken when new information technology appears, and that balancing has been identified as one of the functions of government by the neoclassical school of economics [55]. The development of digital copyright under cloud computing environment cannot rely on private funding only, and the technical strength and stakeholders themselves cannot solve coordination issues. Besides, the Chinese digital copyright market is not mature enough and still needs government involvement.

As the main pillar of market surveillance and public service provider, government can improve the development and standardization of the digital copyright market by using cloud computing technology right from the public policy formulation level to the industry management level, all within the public welfare as the norm of government participation.

4.2   Public Policy Formulation

The government can improve digital copyright statutory license system in three ways: first, by defining the commonwealth cultural project clearly; second, by further exerting the advantage of statutory license announcement system and by further strengthening government's function of formulating public policies to solve digital copyright issues in non-profit cultural undertakings; and third, by further classifying the types of digital copyright in statutory license. The traditional "copy" concept has been considered to strangle the diffusion of information resources in digital environment while cloud computing further supports dissemination and usage of digital information resources so that scholars can come up with various attempts to reconstruct the copyright system [54] such as communication-centralized rights theory, commercial use rights model, and work access rights model, which are all beneficial and inspiring attempts [56].

Government purchases, administrative allocation and coordination are still important ways for government to participate in the digital copyright market. In the cloud computing environment, ways of resource usage may change to hire-based and demand-based, thus it is necessary to adjust public finance policies for digital rights purchase, allocation and coordination mechanisms. In the meantime, from the long-term view, we can make full use of the cloud service such as Copyright Cloud digital copyright integration platform to solve copyright authorization and licensing issues through purchase of copyright agent service.

It is necessary for government to develop cloud computing security laws and regulations to clarify the responsibilities of each party so as to make explicit the legal responsibilities and obligations between cloud service providers and users. The government should also establish security audit system of cloud computing for regular security comprehensive assessment to improve transparency of its internal operation and ensure reliability [57].

4.3   Enhancement of Digital Copyright Industry Management

Government can promote digital copyright industry chain integration by exploiting cloud computing technologies, integrating existing copyright management agencies such as the China Written Works Copyright Society, China Music Copyright Society, and others to achieve transparent management and transaction of copyright.

Besides promotion of industry chain integration, the government can also develop national standards for digital licensing and cloud computing as soon as possible. Meanwhile, the government needs to advocate developing independent digital licensing standards for intellectual property [58].

Strengthening digital copyright market regulation is another way for government to promote digital copyright market in the cloud computing environment. Cloud computing technology makes storage, transmission, usage and payment of copyright works different from the existing model, and it can be easy to find copyright leaks and harm the interests of copyright owners and users [17], [59]. We recommend that the National Copyright Administration pay full attention to the cloud computing technology development during the construction of Network Copyright Monitoring Platform and consolidate supervision of digital copyright licensing market using cloud computing technology.

5   Conclusion

In addition to the formulation of relevant laws and regulations, the development of copyright strategies, digital rights market regulation, copyright advocacy and education, the government is also actively involved in the digital copyright permission from different sources in China as we mentioned above.

Through the funding of public cultural information sharing project and the national digital library, the government uses national purchasing, administrative coordination, copyright collecting, society donations, and other ways to obtain the authorization of the copyright, and this government participation results in the use of fewer resources and lowers the cost of providing the quality and efficiency of public services.

References

1. The Copyright Law of the People's Republic of China (2010), http://www.wipo.int/wipolex/en/text.jsp?file_id=186569
2. National Copyright Administration of the People's Republic of China, http://www.ncac.gov.cn/
3. China Internet Network Information Center, http://www.cnnic.cn
4. Research Center of Chinese E-business, http://www.100ec.cn
5. Ma, J.: Network Writing and National Culture Strategy. People's Daily (Overseas Edition) (February 1, 2010)
6. Hu, A.G., Wang, S.G.: Government and Market. China Planning, Beijing (1999)
7. Li, R.: Ethical Analysis of Government Intervention in the Market. Chinese Academy of Social Sciences, Beijing (2001)
8. Xu, F.: Study of Indirect Infringement Liability of Internet Copyright: From the Point of United States Law. Fudan University, Shanghai (2011)

9. Qin, X., Hu, Z.Q.: Analysis of Copyright Protection in Digital Era. Editor's Friend 12, 101–103 (2010)
10. Nie, S.H.: China Written Works Copyright Society: Establishing Digital Copyright Authentication Mechanism. China Intellectual Property 38 (2010)
11. Paul, T.J., Lin, J., Justin, M.G.: Cloud Computing and Information Policy: Computing in a Policy Cloud? Journal of Information Technology and Politics 5, 269–283 (2008)
12. He, Y.J.: Mobile Internet Service Delivery Model Based on Cloud Computing. Post Design Technology 10, 39–42 (2011)
13. Gao, F., Zhang, Q., Li, Z.Q.: Cloud Platform Construction of Film and Television Programs Based on Cloud Computing Technology. Cloud Computing Application in Broadcast and Television 7, 3–38 (2012)
14. Fu, X.W.: Analysis of the Security Issues in Cloud Computing Mode. Computer CD Software and Applications 5, 106–107 (2012)
15. He, Y.J.: Mobile Internet Service Delivery Model Based on Cloud Computing. Post Design Technology 10, 39–42 (2011)
16. Wang, X.L.: Theory and Application of Cloud Computing. Silicon Valley 9, 24–25 (2012)
17. Hu, X.P.: Visualization of Cloud Library. The Theory and Research of Intelligence 6, 29–32 (2010)
18. Liu, Y.Q., Liu, J.L., Chen, Z.R., Wang, Z.Y.: Copyright Management and Countermeasure under the Cloud Computing Technology Conditions. Publishing Research 2, 73–76 (2012)
19. Wang, Z.Q.: Should not Exaggerate the Influence of New Technology on Copyright. China Press and Publishing Journal, http://www.Chinaxwcb.com/2011-11/24/content_233574.htm
20. Goldsmith, A.A.: The State, the Market and Economic Development: A Second Look at Adam Smith in Theory and Practice. Development and Change 26, 633–650 (1995)
21. Werhane, P.: Adam Smith and His Legacy for Modern Capitalism. Oxford University, New York (1991)
22. Skinner, A.A.: A System of Social Science. Oxford University, Oxford (1979)
23. Smith, A.: Lectures on Jurisprudence. Oxford University, Oxford (1978)
24. North, D., Thomas, R.: The Rise of the Western World: A New Economic History. Cambridge University, New York (1973)
25. Keynes, M.J.: The General Theory of Employment, Interest, and Money. Harcourt, San Diego (1991)
26. Liu, G.Z.: The Comparison of Adam Smith and Keynes's Views about the Government's Economic Duty. Hebei University, Baoding (2006)
27. Zhao, Z.H.: Where is the Boundary of the Government and Market. Liberation Daily, http://theory.gmw.cn/2012-12/19/content_6072911.htm
28. Rong, J.: How to Summarize the Over Three Decades Revolution of China?, http://view.news.qq.com/a/20130425/000030_all.htm
29. Zeng, X.M.: Concerning the Copyright Market Cultivation and Development of Copyright Agent. China Publishing Journal 2, 23–24 (2008)
30. Gou, J.Z.: The Government Responsibility in the Copyright Trade. Theory Study 7, 17–19 (2008)

31. Zhu, L.P.: Perfection of the Government Regulation on Internet Copyright. The North Economy and Trade 5, 53 (2010)
32. Subashini, S., Kavitha, V.: A Survey on Security Issues in Service Delivery Models of Cloud Computing. Journal of Network and Computer Applications 34, 1–11 (2011)
33. Zhang, P.: Digital Publishing Need to Improve Copyright Authorization Model. Beijing Business Today (2011)
34. Zhou, L.: Cloud Computing Technology Protecting Digital Copyright. Suzhou University, Suzhou (2012)
35. Paul, T.J., Lin, J., Justin, M.G.: Cloud Computing and Information Policy: Computing in a Policy Cloud? Journal of Information Technology and Politics 5, 269–283 (2008)
36. Cloud Computing Challenges Existing Copyright Law, http://szsb.sznews.com
37. The China Copyright Protection Center, http://www.ccopyright.com.cn
38. "Five in One" Development China Digital Publishing, http://news.xinhuanet.com
39. Introducing Cloud Computing into Digital Rights Circulation Field in Our Country, http://www.dzwww.com
40. Copyright Cloud Builds New Rights Circulation Environment, http://www.bookdao.com
41. Mobile Reading Copyright Self-help Settlement Platform has been on the Internet, http://edit.hongxiu.com/zhuanti/document/view.asp?id=3196
42. National Digital Culture Network, http://www.ndcnc.gov.cn
43. The Basic Training Materials for the Villages and Towns Service Station. National Cultural Information Resource Construction Management Center (2009)
44. Fu, P.: The Construction of National Library Digital Resource. Journal of the National Library 4, 24–27 (2004)
45. Li, H.W.: The Rights Management of National Library Digital Resources, Construction and Service. Forum of Digital Library 8, 43–48 (2008)
46. Lawrence, B.: The "Public Use" Requirement in Eminent Domain. Oregon Law Review 57, 1–47 (1978)
47. Richard, A.P.: Economic Analysis of Law. Encyclopedia of China Publishing, Beijing (1997)
48. Article 9 of Regulation on the Protection of the Right to Network Dissemination of Information, http://www.wipo.int/wipolex/en/text.jsp?file_id=182147
49. Zhou, P.: The Copyright Protection of Digital Media Products Based on Cloud Computing, http://www.tv1926.com/bencandy-90-193414-2.htm
50. Li, Y.T.: The Discussion of Digital Copyright of Compulsory License and its Introduction from the Perspective of Administration. China Publishing Journal 2, 42–45 (2013)
51. The Central People's Government of P.R.C., http://www.gov.cn/zxft/ft60/content_751981.htm
52. Zhou, Z.: Government Purchase of Public Services and Reference and Enlightenment of Developed Countries. Western Financial Accounting 5, 14–18 (2008)
53. Introduction of Digital Library of China, http://www.cdlc.cn/about/about.aspx

54. Wang, W.G.: Function Study of the Government Procurement Policy 2009. Doctoral thesis of Institute of Fiscal Science (2009)
55. Wu, H.D., Xiao, Y.D.: Network Dissemination Rights and Fair Use in Digital Era. Technology and Law 4, 39–58 (2004)
56. Diao, S.X.: Problems and Suggestions of Construction of Copyright Law Rule: From the Perspective of Cloud Computing. China Soft Science 1, 13–23 (2013)
57. Feng, D.G., Zhang, M., Zhang, Y., Xu, Z.: Study on Cloud Computing Security. Journal of Software 22, 71–83 (2011)
58. Jia, Y.W., Zhao, D., Jiang, K.Y., Luan, G.C.: The Cloud Computing Strategy of the United States Federal Government. E-Government 7, 2–6 (2011)
59. Dong, X.X., Lu, T.J.: Review of the Cloud Computing Study and Its Future Development. Journal of Beijing Post University (Social Sciences Edition) 5, 80 (2010)

Click Here to Cloud: End User Issues in Cloud Computing Terms of Service Agreements

Tomas A. Lipinski

School of Library and Information Science, Kent State University,
314 Library, 1125 Risman Drive,
Kent, Ohio 44242-001
tlipins1@kent.edu

Abstract. Four Terms of Service (TOS) agreements offered by commercial providers of cloud computing services are reviewed in order to identify those provisions that are problematic from the perspective of the end user. The following services were reviewed: iCloud, OpenDrive, Dropbox and Amazon Cloud Drive. The legality of the mass-market licenses is assessed. Specific provisions are reviewed with the goal of understanding the consequences on the user/consumer of cloud computing services; particularly those provisions that may result in unintended or detrimental consequences for users/consumers are identified. The effect of the law of contract (license) is contrasted with the law of copyright. Recommendations are made throughout the discussion to improve TOS provisions for the end user. Developments in the law of contract are surveyed to determine the enforceability of specific provisions as well as the potential avenues of challenge to problematic clauses discussing whether such clauses might be unconscionable.

Keywords: Contract law, copyright law, license terms and conditions, unintended consequences, public policy, unconscionability.

1 Introduction

Cloud computing services agreements are governed by contract law as the cloud computing service is licensed to the user. A license is simply a form of legal permission. The consequences for cloud computing users are significant. These agreements are often referred to as Terms of Service (TOS) or End User Licensing Agreements (EULAs). Through these agreements the user is obtaining permission to access and use "the cloud." The user is not obtaining a physical object such as a book, rather is acquiring use of a service. Unlike a purchase, where the buyer may come to own the product such as DVD, licensees do not possess ownership rights in the cloud service nor is such service perpetual. As there is no transfer of a physical item, the license of cloud services means that contract law governs the acquisition of the service and its subsequent use. Using contract law allows a service provider to ignore in a sense the default of rules of copyright that would otherwise apply to the use of content protected by copyright such as literary works (a book or a computer program)

J.N. Gathegi et al. (Eds.): IMCW 2013, CCIS 423, pp. 92–111, 2014.
© Springer-Verlag Berlin Heidelberg 2014

or an audiovisual work (a motion picture on a DVD). In the cloud computing environment the cloud operating software, the content a cloud service provider makes available to users and most important to the cloud user, as well as content stored by a user in the cloud fall often within the subject matter of copyright protection. However, other provisions in the TOS may take away use rights that would otherwise be available if the copyright law alone applied. In this way, contract law trumps copyright law.

The cloud TOS also establish other operating rules governing use of the service, including the obligations and responsibilities of each party. Moreover cloud license provisions can further elaborate how disputes will be settled, limit damages and otherwise reallocate risk among the parties. Often providers of web based services including cloud space disavow any responsibility for loss of user content or accuracy of content the provider might make available. The legal concept involved here is a waiver of warranty. A license therefore allows the service provider to shift legal risk entirely onto the user. Requiring users to indemnify the service provider further accomplishes this objective, often with unintended consequences or results for the user. Cloud computing services are not subject to negotiation and so there the user is faced with a take-it-or-leave-it scenario of either accepting the provisions of the license in total or foregoing use of the service. This paper analyzes the text of four common cloud computing TOS: iCloud, OpenDrive, Dropbox and Amazon Cloud Drive. The version of each agreement used in this assessment is that version available to the author on Sunday May 19, 2013. Each license was analyzed in detail, provision by provision. That analysis is too lengthy to include here but a summary table of the most significant license variables reflected in the TOS provisions is presented at the end of the discussion. If readers are interested in the provision-by-provision commentary the author is able to provide that assessment upon contact.

Several questions are posed in the context of United States copyright law and general notions of U.S. contract law. What mechanisms make such TOS binding upon the user? Are there other unintended consequences for users such as a limitation on other rights or imposition of burdensome obligations? Are there particular provisions that take away rights that users would otherwise have in the absence of the TOS, i.e., that users would have if the transaction was subject to the copyright law? Finally, is legal challenge to these consequences ever possible?

2   Legality: Contract Formation Issues

In the world of web site access, "use" equates with "agreement" or in contract parlance "assent" to the terms that govern the space the same as if the user placed their signature on a legal document. In *Register.com, Inc. v. Verio, Inc.*, the court concluded that use of the Register.com search service constituted the requisite legal assent to form a valid contract: "by proceeding to submit a WHOIS query, Verio manifested its assent to be bound by Register.com's terms of use and a contract was formed and subsequently breached" [1]. While web based contracts are then in theory valid there should be an opportunity to read the TOS prior to agreement and a clear mechanism for assent to those terms such as a click-here-to-agree mechanism. In cloud space environments the TOS are readily available for review by prospective and current users. However, cloud services like many other web sites adopt a strategy expressed in its TOS that use of the web site or in this case, use of the cloud space, equates to assent with the TOS. With the exception of iCloud the TOS reviewed equate use of the service with assent. This raises obvious problems not only regarding initial contract formation but in change of terms, notice, etc. The reason that use-equals-assent provisions are problematic is that it becomes difficult to know when use indeed means assent or use is just that, regular use of the cloud service. Divining assent from conduct that one would expect with a web service is not wise from the perspective of a user as mere use could represent assent to terms that have changed, acceptance of additional charges or increased pricing schemes, etc. How is use of the service (an expected course of conduct) to be distinguished from assent? As discussed below the mechanism for changing the TOS exacerbates this problem. After terms have been changed by the cloud provider a user might log into their cloud service without realizing the terms have changed. However since use equates to assent, the user has unknowingly just agreed to those changes in the terms.

Table 1. Change in terms provisions in cloud computing TOS

TOS Provision	iCloud	OpenDrive	Dropbox	Amazon Cloud Drive
Change in Terms Provisions in Cloud Computing	"Apple reserves the right to modify or terminate the Service (or any part thereof), either temporarily or permanently. Apple may **post** on our website and/or will send an **email** to the primary address associated with your Account to **provide notice of any material changes** to the Service. It is *your responsibility to check* your iCloud email address and/or primary email address registered with Apple for any such notices… Your *continued use* of the Service will be *deemed acceptance* of such modifications and additional terms and conditions."	"OpenDrive reserves the right to modify the terms and conditions of this Agreement or its policies relating to the Service at any time, **effective upon posting of an updated version of this Agreement on the Service.** *You are responsible for regularly reviewing* this Agreement. Continued *use* of the Service after any such changes shall *constitute* your *consent* to such changes."	"We may revise these Terms from time to time and **the most current version will always be posted on our website**. If a **revision**, in **our sole discretion**, is **material** we will **notify you** (for example via email to the **email** address associated with your account). Other changes may be **posted to our blog** or terms page, so *please check those pages regularly*. By continuing to *access or use* the Services after revisions become effective, *you agree to be bound* by the revised Terms."	"We may amend the Agreement at our **sole discretion** **by posting** the revised terms in the **Service or on Amazon.com**, but any increase in fees will not affect the cost of your Service Plan during its term. Your *continued use* of the Service or the Software after any amendment evidences your *agreement to be bound* by it."

How is the user to know of such change before accessing their cloud space? Notice would accomplish this, but the user would still need to figure which terms changed. Proper notice then should not only alert the user to a change but indicate the term or terms that have changed and include a mechanism for acceptance, e.g., click-to-agree. The four cloud services reviewed differ in approach with iCloud and Dropbox providing notice of material changes via email to the user. There may still be an issue regarding what the provider versus the user believes are material terms for which notice should be provided. A material term is one that goes to the heart of the bargain or agreement. Price is an example of a material term. For the cloud user a significant change in storage capacity might also be material.

The other two cloud providers, OpenDrive and Amazon Cloud Drive, simply post the changes to their websites. A user would need to be vigilant by checking the date of the last update to see if there has been a recent change then compare the TOS in effect previously (remember to save a copy for easy access) with the newly posted TOS to see what has changed. Users need to be aware of the consequences when terms can change without notice and use equates to assent to those changes. It is questionable whether an approach such as "check our website for changes" is a legally valid mechanism for purposes of assent to those changes. In mass market agreement scenarios such as those for cloud services, where every customer gets the same TOS, at least one federal appellate court indicated that using a "check our website for changes" mechanism is indeed not valid. The United States Court of Appeals for the Ninth Circuit in *Douglas v. Talk America, Inc.* [2], concluded that posting of changes followed by use of service is not enforceable. "Talk America posted the revised contract on its website but, according to Douglas, it never notified him that the contract had changed. Unaware of the new terms, Douglas continued using Talk America's services for four years" [3]. The court concluded that the new terms were not part of the agreement: "Even if Douglas had visited the website, he would have had no reason to look at the contract posted there. Parties to a contract have no obligation to check the terms on a periodic basis to learn whether they have been changed by the other side" [4]. Once a contract is formed any changes represent an offer for additional terms, an offer that in theory requires separate and distinct assent. The court further commented on the problem of providing notice unless the notice also identifies which terms changed: "Nor would a party know *when* to check the website for possible changes to the contract terms without being notified that the contract has been changed and how. Douglas would have had to check the contract every day for possible changes. Without notice, an examination would be fairly cumbersome, as Douglas would have had to compare every word of the posted contract with his existing contract in order to detect whether it had changed" [5]. Although iCloud uses a click-to-agree mechanism for initial contract formation all of TOS reviewed here adopt a use-after-posting-equals-assent approach for changes in terms. It is determined that the agreements examined raise contract formation and assent issues.

3   The Impact of TOS in the Cloud Environment: Unintended Consequences

The TOS establish the operating rules of the service, including the obligations and responsibilities of each party towards each other and other users. The TOS do much more than this however. The provisions can further elaborate how disputes will be settled, limit damages and reallocate risk among the parties. First, all of the four cloud providers disclaim various warranties regarding the availability of their respective service and any harm a user might suffer from loss of service. Worse, three of the services (all but Dropbox) require the user to indemnify the provider for any harm suffered due to conduct of the user. For example if a user stored infringing content a copyright owner could sue the user but could also sue the service provider under a theory of contributory copyright infringement. Indemnifications have serious legal consequences.   If a provider were found liable for contributory copyright infringement the user would be obligated to cover the loss (damages) suffered by the service provider; this is the power of an indemnification.

The TOS may also limit the form of remedy the user may pursue. Amazon Cloud Drive requires the parties to use arbitration, with users forced to waive their right to participate in a class action suit against the provider. This can be a significant deterrent for individual users seeking redress. In addition, so-called boilerplate provisions can be problematic. Such provisions are common to many contracts. Choice of law and choice of forum are two examples. A user seeking judicial remedy would be forced to litigate in the home state of the service provider and use the law of that state. A non-waiver provision is another boilerplate provision and allows the service provider discretion in deciding against which users it will enforce the TOS. A non-waiver provision requires that a waiver of an enforcement right of the service provider must be in writing; it cannot be based on conduct alone, i.e., non-enforcement against another user.

3.1   Termination and Suspension Rights of the Service Provider

In cloud computing environments termination provisions are also very important. While it is not uncommon for the contractual relationship to end at some point one consideration is whether adequate notice is provided if the service provider intends to terminate the user's access from his or her cloud and whether suspension of services is also possible. All of the TOS reviewed restrict in some way the content a user can post, store, distribute to other users, etc. These restrictions are typically broad. While some restrictions forbid content that is unlawful such as obscene material or defamatory content other prohibitions restrict content that is perfectly lawful in the United States such as hate speech. Some categories of restricted content are without legal meaning or are undefined in the TOS such as "otherwise objectionable" content. This results in problems interpreting the provision. What iCloud may deem "otherwise objectionable" may not be to a particular user. Dropbox is the least restrictive forbidding only content that is infringing (of copyright) or harmful to the system ("spyware or any other malicious software"). If a user violates the content prohibition the cloud provider can terminate the user. iCloud: can terminate for "(a) violations of this Agreement or any other policies or guidelines that are referenced herein and/or posted on the Service." OpenDrive also has a similar prerogative: "OpenDrive, in its sole discretion, may terminate your password, account or use of the Service and remove and discard any Data within the Service if you fail to comply with this Agreement." The Dropbox TOS allows for either suspension or termination: "For example, we may suspend or terminate your use if you are not complying with these Terms, or use the Services in any way that would cause us legal liability or

Table 2. Termination and suspension provisions in cloud computing TOS

TOS Provision	iCloud	OpenDrive	Dropbox	Amazon Cloud Drive
Termination And Suspension Provisions in Cloud Computing	"If your use of the Service or other **behavior** intentionally or unintentionally **threatens** Apple's ability to provide the Service or other systems, Apple shall be entitled to take all reasonable steps to protect the Service and Apple's systems, which may include **suspension** of your access to the Service. Repeated violations of the limitations may result in **termination** of your Account… Apple may at any time, under certain circumstances and *without prior notice* , **immediately terminate or suspend** all or a portion of your Account and/or access to the Service."	"OpenDrive, in its *sole discretion*, may **terminate** your password, account or use of the Service and remove and discard any Data within the Service if you *fail to comply* with this Agreement."	"Though we'd much rather you stay, you can stop using our Services any time. We reserve the right to suspend or end the Services at *any time, with or without cause*, and with or without notice. For example, we may **suspend or terminate** your use if you are *not complying with these Terms*, or use the Services in any way that would cause us legal liability or disrupt others' use of the Services."	"Your rights under the Agreement will automatically **terminate** without notice if you *fail to comply with its terms*. We may terminate the Agreement or restrict, **suspend** or **terminate** your use of the Service at our discretion *without notice at any time*, including if we determine that your *use violates the Agreement*, is improper, substantially exceeds or differs from normal use by other users, or otherwise involves fraud or misuse of the Service or harms our interests or those of another user of the Service."

One of the most important provisions from the user's perspective—the main reason for going to the cloud—is that a user can store, then access their content. If the user can either be subject to denial of access through termination or suspension or have their content removed from the service the concept of "in the cloud" becomes less useful. Yet this is precisely what all four cloud TOS indicate can happen. Removal of content is discussed below when it reflects a response to claims of infringing content. But loss of content can be also result when the user is terminated or their use suspended. Suffice it to say that cloud providers have broad discretion to terminate a user. All TOS examined also have the right to suspend access as well. Termination or suspension can come at anytime without notice. It is more typical in contract law to condition a termination right on a breach of a material term by the non-terminating party, where termination is preceded by notice and an opportunity to cure the breach. Here the cloud providers have broad discretion to terminate and suspend a user from the service. Apple iCloud can terminate if the user "threatens Apple's ability to provide the service." The remaining providers can terminate if a user is not complying with the TOS, though DropBox can terminate "at any time, with or without cause." In addition, Apple iCloud can terminate if the user does not keep their account information accurate (how Apple would know this is unclear).

Table 3. Content and conduct restrictions in cloud computing TOS

TOS Provision	iCloud	OpenDrive	Dropbox	Amazon Cloud Drive
Content/ Conduct Restriction Provisions in Cloud Computing	"You agree that you will NOT use the Service to: a. upload, download, post, email, transmit, store or otherwise make available any Content that is unlawful, harassing, threatening, harmful, tortious, defamatory, libelous, *abusive*, violent, obscene, *vulgar*, invasive of another's privacy, **hateful**, racially or ethnically offensive, or **otherwise objectionable** … d. **pretend to be anyone, or any entity, you are not** — you may not impersonate or misrepresent yourself as another person (including celebrities), entity, another iCloud user, an Apple employee, or a civic or government leader, or otherwise misrepresent your affiliation with a person or entity… e. engage in any copyright infringement or other intellectual property infringement (including uploading any content to which you do not have the right to upload), or disclose any trade secret or confidential information in violation of a confidentiality, employment, or nondisclosure agreement… i. interfere with or disrupt the Service (including accessing the Service through any automated means, like scripts or web crawlers), or any servers or networks connected to the Service, or any policies, requirements or regulations of networks connected to the Service (including any unauthorized access to, use or monitoring of data or traffic thereon)…"	"You agree to abide by all applicable local, state, national and foreign laws, treaties and regulations in connection with the Service… you agree not to use the Service to:… (b) harvest, collect, gather or assemble information or data regarding other users, including e-mail addresses, without their consent; (c) transmit through or post on the Service unlawful, **harassing**, libelous, **abusive**, harassing, tortious, defamatory, threatening, harmful, libelous, invasive of another's privacy, **vulgar**, obscene or **otherwise objectionable material of** any kind or nature or which is harmful to minors in any way; (d) transmit any material that may infringe the intellectual property rights or other rights of third parties, including trademark, copyright or right of publicity; … or (h) harass or **interfere with another user's** use and **enjoyment of the Service**."	"Files and other content in the Services may be protected by intellectual property rights of others. Please do not copy, upload, download, or share files unless you have the right to do so. You, not Dropbox, will be fully responsible and liable for what you copy, share, upload, download or otherwise use while using the Services… You must not upload spyware or any other malicious software to the Service."	"You may only share Your Files in which you have all necessary copyright and other rights… You are solely responsible for how you share Your Files and who may access Your Files that you share. You may not share files (a) that contain defamatory, threatening, **abusive**, pornographic, or **otherwise objectionable** material, (b) that advocate **bigotry**, **hatred**, or illegal discrimination, or (c) if sharing those files violates any law, any intellectual property…"

disrupt others' use of the Services." A similar suspension or termination right appears in the Amazon Cloud Drive TOS: "We may terminate the Agreement or restrict, suspend or terminate your use of the Service at our discretion without notice at any time, including if we determine that your use violates the Agreement, is improper, substantially exceeds or differs from normal use by other users, or otherwise involves fraud or misuse of the Service or harms our interests or those of another user of the Service." None of the TOS reviewed indicate the difference between termination and suspension and in the case of suspension how long the period of suspension will last. In general the breach of a content restriction can result in harsh action, loss of content, termination or suspension.

3.2   A Lesson from the AOL Litigation and Enforcing Content Restrictions

While the TOS impose content and conduct restrictions on cloud users such provisions do not vest users with enforcement rights against other users, i.e., if another user posts "otherwise objectionable" or "abusive" content for example, a user cannot legally force the cloud provider to remove it. In *Noah v. America Online, Inc.* [6], a subscriber brought an unsuccessful claim that AOL "wrongfully refused to prevent participants in an online chat room from posting or submitting harassing comments that blasphemed and defamed plaintiff's Islamic religion and his co-religionists" [7]. The claim was barred by the immunity of 47 U.S.C. § 230 because the claim "seeks to treat AOL as the publisher of the allegedly harassing statements of other AOL members" [8]. The court concluded that TOS provisions regarding online comportment and civility (the AOL "Community Guidelines") created no contractual duty on the part of AOL, rather the "plain language of the Member Agreement makes clear that AOL is not obligated to take any action" [9].

3.3   Risk Shifting Strategies by Cloud Service Providers

Another striking provision is the indemnification that three services (all but Dropbox) require a user to provide to the cloud service provider. An indemnification provision in a TOS represents the user's legal promise to compensate the provider for loss or damage sustained by it due to the conduct of the user. As the *Noah v. America Online, Inc.* decision indicates, federal statute provides immunity for any "provider or user of an interactive computer service" from harms arising from "any information provided by another information content provider." 47 U.S.C. § 230(c)(1). Further, under the copyright law, 17 U.S.C. § 512, a limitation on liability exists for infringing copyright content posted by subscribers. All four cloud service providers are registered with the U.S. Copyright Office as section 512 service providers with provisions, discussed below, that reflect this status. Arguably, indemnification of the service provider by the user is not needed. It is argued that in light of these two statutory protections an indemnification is the legal equivalent of "overkill." Use of an indemnification provision is one way the cloud provider attempts to shift the legal risk of the parties. In the absence of such provisions the law generally places risk across the responsible parties; here most if not all of that risk is shifted onto the cloud user.

In addition to indemnification provisions two other provisions help the service provider shift legal risk. First, warranties or guarantees regarding the service are disclaimed. Second, damages are limited or waived altogether. A warranty is a legal promise. In traditional contracts for the sale of goods the buyer expects the product to work. Over time courts have responded to this practical expectation with the legal concept of implied warranty, i.e., the sale of a product implies certain warranties about the condition of the product. The purchaser-consumer expects the product to work and this is expressed in the law as a warranty of merchantability or fitness for a particular purpose. As the contract law developed courts concluded that these buyer expectations were reasonable and applied the warranties of merchantability and fitness to sales of goods. An "implied warranty of fitness for a particular purpose is a warranty implied by law when a seller has reason to know that a buyer wishes goods for a particular purpose and is relying on the seller's skill and judgment to furnish those goods" [10]. A general warranty that the product is ready for the marketplace is an implied warranty of merchantability. A merchantability warranty "means that a good sold carries with it an inherent soundness which makes that good suitable for the purpose for which it was designed" [11].

Likewise it might be expected here by a cloud user that the service will work, i.e., that the service will be available and that content placed in the cloud is secure and available for later access and use. Again contract law through the TOS allows the cloud provider to shift the legal risk of the parties to the transaction, by disclaiming any promise implied or otherwise that the service will work. Taking a lesson from the software industry providers of software realized that promises of bug free or error free software were impractical to make, even if the user expected such promises. As a result, disclaimers were used to make the consumer aware that the product will not be error-free and that the software is made available "as is" with errors and all. Cloud computing services providers have similar concerns and so engage in similar risk-shifting reallocations of legal responsibility. All four providers make their clouds available "as is" with faults, errors, etc. An "as is" warranty is a "warranty that [the] goods are sold with all existing faults" [12]. The "as is" provision indicates to the cloud user that "you take the service as it is with all quirks, bugs, faults, delays, etc." In cloud computing environments this is yet another way in which the cloud service provider shifts legal risk, disclaiming any responsibility for harm it might cause. Each of the cloud computing TOS agreements examined contain a warranty disclaimer. The Amazon Cloud Drive disclaimer however is incorporated by reference to another agreement, Amazon Web Service Customer Agreement where the actual disclaimer provision is located in paragraph 10 of that agreement [13]. In some states certain warranties cannot be waived in consumer contracts and the iCloud, OpenDrive and Dropbox warranty disclaimers provisions include a statement to this effect.

If in spite of numerous warranty disclaimers a court should find the service provider responsible for harm a final strategy that all cloud providers employ is to limit the scope of the damages that can be awarded. Should a court find fault with the service provider the damages would be so minuscule as to discourage any claim from ever being brought. It is typical to limit damages to the cost of the subscription fee.

Such disclaimers are legal, but most jurisdictions require that such disclaimers be conspicuous, thus such disclaimers are often in bold or all capitals.

4   The Impact of Licensed Services on Copyright

Cloud computing TOS may alter the legal landscape of copyright ownership and use rights. Particular provisions may take away rights that users would otherwise have in the absence of the contract, i.e., rights that users would have if the transaction was subject to the copyright law. It is not uncommon for other web-based services such as social network sites to require that users grant the service a non-exclusive right to use content submitted by users. [14] Such provision was not found in the four TOS reviewed here. Moreover, the four cloud computing agreements reviewed for this chapter ensure that a user retains the copyright in his or her content. In the future, a service provider might decide to claim copyright ownership in the content stored by users in the cloud it provides. In order for this to occur the TOS would need to change. As discussed earlier all of the TOS reviewed indicate that use-equals-assent to any changes in terms, so such changes could be easily accomplished.

In addition, each service retains the right through the processes outlined in 17 U.S.C. § 512 to remove content that is claimed to be infringing. If a user posts content to his or her cloud space that a copyright owner claims is infringing the TOS indicate that the service provider will follow the DMCA (Digital Millennium Copyright Act) take-down rules. The rules are codified in 17 U.S.C. § 512. This take-down will occur even if the content is not infringing. The protection a service provider receives from the statute requires the content be removed or disabled "expeditiously." While the take-down statute provides for a process of restoration of content or access none of the TOS reviewed alert users to the possibility of restoration. Under the statute, a restoration request must come from the user whose content was removed or access disabled.

The most significant loss of copyright use rights in many license agreements are those relating to fair use. The iCloud TOS does not allow a user to "reverse engineer, decompile, or otherwise attempt to discover the source code." However several courts have determined that in certain circumstance reverse engineering or decompilation of software can be a fair use under 17 U.S.C. § 107 when it is done to determine the unprotected elements in the software or to achieve interoperability [15] [16][17] [18]. A second right of users often curtailed through software and other licenses is known as the right of first sale. Codified in 17 U.S.C. §109, the first sale doctrine allows the "owner of a particular copy or phonorecord lawfully made under this title" to make a public distribution of the copy or phonorecord without seeking permission from the copyright owner or paying an additional fee. [19] This is the legal mechanism at play when a user buys a book from Amazon, gives it to a friend as a gift, and after reading the book the friend sells it at a yard sale. After paying for the initial copy, users are free to make subsequent distributions (the gift, the yard sale). However, as the cloud service is made available through a license and not a sale, users do not "own" their access to the cloud service. Ownership is a statutory prerequisite before a user can exercise first sale rights. It is also difficult to conceive of first sale rights in virtual environments as a recent court discussing the "reselling" of iTunes files observed: "Put another way the first sale defense is limited to *material items*, like records, that the copyright owner can put in the stream of commerce… Section109(a) still protects a lawful owner's sale of her 'particular' phonorecord, be it a computer *hard disk*, *iPod*, or other *memory device* onto which the file was originally downloaded" [20]. The observation suggests that for device bound software such as a cell phone or e-reader a user might indeed be an owner and have first sale rights in the accompanying software even though those devices are typically made available to consumers through a license with a similar restriction. As there is no physical element to cloud service it would appear that first sale rights would not apply. In the absence of first sale rights a cloud user might want to transfer or assign his or her access rights in their cloud space. However, all four TOS reviewed also prevent the non-assignment of the service to another user.

5   Unconscionability

Proactive users can best approach cloud computing TOS by identifying the various provisions in the governing agreement and understanding the consequence or impact of those provisions in order to better assess the desirability of one service over another. A reactive approach is one where once faced with an undesirable consequence or impact of a provision a user may attempt to have a court conclude that the provision is void. One legal vehicle for this determination is to request that a court rule the provision unenforceable because it is unconscionable. The determination of unconscionability is a matter of law for the court to decide and is made on a case by case basis. A court can void the entire agreement (if the entire contract is unconscionable), strike a particular clause or clauses and leave the remainder of the contract intact sans the offending language or leave the language as drafted but limit the application of the clause(s) so as to rectify the unconscionable effect.

There are two aspects to the concept of unconscionability: procedural unconscionability and substantive unconscionability. A number of courts require that both elements be present before a provision or an entire contract is deemed unconscionable. "The procedural component is satisfied by the existence of unequal bargaining positions and hidden terms common in the context of adhesion contracts. The substantive component is satisfied by overly harsh or one-sided results that 'shock the conscience'" [21]. Cloud computing TOS are not subject to negotiation so the user is faced with a take-it-or-leave-it scenario choice of either accepting the provisions of the license in total or foregoing use of the service. Such contracts are known as adhesion contracts and satisfy the first element of procedural unconscionability. An adhesion contract is a "standard-form contract prepared by one party, to be signed by another party in a weaker position, usually a consumer, who adheres to the contract with little choice about the terms" [22]. The question remains whether the element of substantive unconscionability is present. Until 2011, one state court held that a class action waiver and mandatory arbitration was per se unconscionable but that result is now foreclosed by the United States Supreme Court decision in *AT&T Mobility LLC v. Concepcion* [23]. Only Amazon Cloud Drive contains an arbitration provision ("Any dispute or claim arising from or relating to the Agreement or the Service is subject to the binding arbitration"). Such provisions must now be examined in light of the Supreme Court decision and based on that assessment the Amazon Cloud Drive arbitration provision appears enforceable. Other provisions have been found to be unconscionable, such as provisions for unreasonably large liquidated damages, or limitations on a debtor's right to redeem collateral [24], but these provisions do not appear in the TOS reviewed here. Clauses waiving remedy for economic loss are also upheld. Recall that all four TOS reviewed have some form of damage limitation. In general there does not appear to be a provision in the TOS reviewed that would be unconscionable as far as courts have thus far articulated the doctrine. However, the doctrine is evolving. It may be that as licensors push the envelope of obligations, restrictions, etc., upon users, courts will respond and expand the list of unconscionable terms. It is clear that cloud computing licenses like consumer software agreements are contracts of adhesion as there is no opportunity to negotiate. The services are presented in a take-it-or-leave environment establishing the first element of procedural unconscionability. This alone does not make such agreements unconscionable as the substantive element is not present in the TOS.

Table 4. Comparison and summary of cloud computing TOS

	iCloud	OpenDrive	Dropbox	Amazon Cloud Drive
Formation and Terminatio n Provisions: *Contract Formation and Assent*	Rather than a use equals assent, there is reference to a click-to-agree mechanism. Users must be over the age of 12, an issue of contractual capacity of sorts, but this would exist with users up to the age of 18. Changes in the terms can be made at any time, without notice, use of the service after changes equals assent to changes in the terms.	Use equal assent. Use equals authority to enter contracts on behalf of organization. Users must have the capacity to contract (be an adult). Use after posted change equals assent.	Use equals assent. Use equals authority to enter contracts on behalf of organization. Authority to contract ("it's your responsibility to ensure that you have the rights or permission needed to comply with these Terms").	Use equals assent.

Table 4. (*Continued*)

Formation and Termination Provisions: *Renewal*	**Evergreen (annual billing date).**	**Monthly fees are deducted automatically.**	None.	**Evergreen. Notify before renewal period.**
Formation and Termination Provisions: *Termination*	Apple can terminate its service. Suspension or termination may occur if account information is not kept accurate, current and complete or a user interferes with Apple's ability to provide its service. In compliance with the DMCA, Apple will terminate a repeat infringer of another's copyright.	Termination upon breach of any term. If termination occurs, a user may obtain their data, but user must pay a fee for it. Upon termination OpenDrive has "no obligation to maintain any Data stored in your account or to forward any Data to you or any third party" a user can request his or her data for a fee but no promise that it will be available.	Termination or suspension can occur at any time for breach of any term or where use "would cause [Dropbox] legal liability or disrupt others' use of the Services." Notice will try but not promise to provide notice of suspension or termination.	"We may change, suspend or discontinue the Service, or any part of it, at any time without notice."
Formation and Termination Provisions: *Suspension*	See above.	Suspension can occur if attempted automatic charge is refused by the user's credit card company. No notice is provided that this has occurred and the user's service may then be "suspended, archived or purged."	See above.	Right to "restrict, suspend or terminate" use without notice if use violates agreement, is "improper", there is excessive use ("substantially exceeds or differs from normal use by other users"), or involves fraud or misuse.

Table 4. (*Continued*)

Formation and Termination Provisions: *Refund*	No refund unless Apple terminates its service (as opposed to terminating a user (see below) except within a narrow window (upgrades within 15 days and 45 days for annual renewal.	No refund for services charged. No refund for extra features ordered then cancelled. No refund if a user terminates (assumes this is the result if OpenDrive terminates as well).	None.	No refund for payments made. Refund if service ceases to exist.
Legal Obligations and Risk Shifting Provisions: *Warranty*	Apple waives any warranty of content stored on its system from damage, corruption, loss or removal and it will not be liable for any damage, corruption, loss or removal. This is repeated in a later provision: Apple "does not guarantee or warrant that any Content you may store or access through the Service will not be subject to inadvertent damage, corruption or loss." Apple makes "no representation that the Service, or any feature or part thereof, is appropriate or available for use in any particular location." Apple does not warrant the content at sites to which it provides links nor is Apple responsible for any damages incurred through use of linked sites or content. There is a specific disclaimer of warranty provision, "as is" and other warranties are disclaimed: "DISCLAIM ALL WARRANTIES OF ANY KIND, WHETHER EXPRESS OR IMPLIED, INCLUDING BUT NOT LIMITED TO THE IMPLIED WARRANTIES OF MERCHANTABILITY, FITNESS FOR A PARTICULAR PURPOSE, AND NON-INFRINGEMENT".	Waiver of liability for "correspondence, purchase or promotion between you and any such third-party" and for linked sites. Disclaimer of warranty related to quality of the service or content. Waiver of other warranties of sale such as merchantability, fitness, etc. Most important OpenDrive disclaims that content provided is free from infringement ("OR NON-INFRINGEMENT OF THIRD PARTY RIGHTS"). The service and content is provided "as is."	"We are not responsible for the accuracy, completeness, appropriateness, or legality of files, user posts, or any other information you may be able to access using the Services." "Dropbox will not be liable for any loss or corruption of your stuff, or for any costs or expenses associated with backing up or restoring any of your stuff." "THE SERVICES AND SOFTWARE ARE PROVIDED "AS IS", AT YOUR OWN RISK, WITHOUT EXPRESS OR IMPLIED WARRANTY OR CONDITION OF ANY KIND. WE ALSO DISCLAIM ANY WARRANTIES OF MERCHANTABILITY, FITNESS FOR A PARTICULAR PURPOSE OR NON-INFRINGEMENT."	Incorporated by 10, Amazon Web Service Customer Agreement. Service is "PROVIDED 'AS IS '" and "DISCLAIM ALL WARRANTIES, INCLUDING ANY IMPLIED WARRANTIES OF MERCHANTA BILITY, SATISFACTO RY QUALITY, FITNESS FOR A PARTICULAR PURPOSE, NON-INFRINGEME NT, OR QUIET ENJOYMENT, AND ANY WARRANTIES ARISING OUT OF ANY COURSE OF DEALING OR USAGE OF TRADE."

Table 4. (*Continued*)

Legal Obligations and Risk Shifting Provisions: *Indemnification*	A user is responsible ("representing" a user is the owner). Apple requires a user to indemnify it from harms resulting from user content, use of the Service, a violation of the agreement, investigation by Apple of agreement violations and violation of any rights of another.	Users are required to indemnify OpenDrive.	None given to users, none required by users.	*Incorporated by 9.1 "You will defend, indemnify, and hold harmless us, our affiliates and licensors, and … their respective employees, officers, directors, and representatives from and against any claims…"
Legal Obligations and Risk Shifting Provisions: *Damage Limitation, Waiver or Disclaimer*	Disclaimer of damages including: "DIRECT, INDIRECT, INCIDENTAL, SPECIAL, CONSEQUENTIAL OR EXEMPLARY DAMAGES, INCLUDING, BUT NOT LIMITED TO, DAMAGES FOR LOSS OF PROFITS, GOODWILL."	Disclaimed, but if not valid damages limited to one month's worth of charges.	Damages limited to $20.00 or three months worth of subscription fees.	Damages limited to cost of service.
Legal Obligations and Risk Shifting Provisions: *Alternative Dispute Resolution— Arbitration*	None.	No arbitration, but the sole remedy is to cease using the service.	None.	Yes.
Legal Obligations and Risk Shifting Provisions: *Boilerplate*	Choice of law, Choice of Forum, Integration, Survivability, Non-assignment, Non-waiver of enforcement.	Choice of Law, Choice of Forum, Agreement of exclusive and personal jurisdiction provision, Integration, Survivability provision, Non-waiver (of enforcement) provision. Non-assignment, but OpenDrive may assign.	Integration, Choice of Law, Choice of Forum, Severability, Non-assignment (by user), Non-waiver (of enforcement).	Non-waiver provision. Non-waiver (of enforcement), Non-assignment, Integration, Choice of law, Choice of forum, Severability located in Amazon Web Service Customer Agreement.

Table 4. (*Continued*)

Content Ownership and Limitations: *Ownership of Copyright*	No ownership in personal identifiers such as Apple ID or email. Apple does not claim ownership of content submitted by a user.	"OpenDrive does not own any data, information or material that you submit to the Service or store in your account ("Data")." "You are the legal owner, representative, or otherwise has a legitimate right to the property or act on the owners behalf and all data contained therein sent to OpenDrive."	"You retain full ownership to your stuff. We don't claim any ownership to any of it."	None stated but the Amazon Web Service Customer Agreement indicates in 8.1 that "between you and us, you or your licensors own all right, title, and interest in and to Your Content."
Content Ownership and Limitations: *Content and Conduct Restrictions*	There are a number of prohibited uses regarding content, some which are protected by law, some are indeed unlawful: "unlawful, harassing, threatening, harmful, tortious, defamatory, libelous, abusive, violent, obscene, vulgar, invasive of another's privacy, hateful, racially or ethnically offensive, or otherwise objectionable"	A long list of content or service exclusions including bulk solicitations, data mining, "unlawful, harassing, libelous, abusive, harassing, tortious, defamatory, threatening, harmful, abusive, libelous, invasive of another's privacy, vulgar, obscene or otherwise objectionable material of any kind or nature or which is harmful to minors in any way" (some of this is lawful content!); infringing, harmful code, robots or other activity harmful to the service, unauthorized access (see 18 U.S.C. § 1030) or "harass or interfere with another user's use and enjoyment of the Service."	Restrictions on infringing or unlawful content ("Please do not copy, upload, download, or share files unless you have the right to do so.") and no "spyware or any other malicious software."	Restrictions on speech protected by the First Amendment. "You may not share files (a) that contain defamatory, threatening, abusive, pornographic, or otherwise objectionable material, (b) that advocate bigotry, hatred, or illegal discrimination, or (c) if sharing those files violates any law, any intellectual property, publicity, privacy, or other right of others, or any license or other agreement by which you are bound."

Table 4. (*Continued*)

Content Ownership and Limitations: *Removal of Content (or make content inaccessible)*	Upon proof of death Apple "may" delete all content. Apple can "pre-screen, move, refuse, modify and/or remove Content at any time, without prior notice and in its sole discretion, if such Content is found to be in violation of this Agreement or is otherwise objectionable." Apple can "modify or change" content in order to "comply with technical requirements of connecting networks or devices or computers."	"We reserve the right to delete or disable content alleged to be infringing and to terminate repeat infringers."	"We may also remove any content from our Services at our discretion."	"If you exceed your Service Plan's storage limit, including by downgrading or not renewing your Service Plan, you may no longer be able to access Your Files."
Content Ownership and Limitations: *DMCA Take-down Process*	Yes.	Yes.	Yes.	Yes.
Use of Service or Content: *Right to Use Subscriber Content*	Users grant Apple a "worldwide, royalty-free, non-exclusive license to use, distribute, reproduce, modify, adapt, publish, translate, publicly perform and publicly display such Content on the Service solely for the purpose for which such Content was submitted or made available, without any compensation or obligation to you."	None stated.	"These Terms do not grant us any rights to your stuff or intellectual property except for the limited rights that are needed to run the Services, as explained below." "You give us the permissions we need to do those things solely to provide the Services," including sharing with third party providers.	"We may use, access, and retain Your Files in order to provide the Service to you and enforce the terms of the Agreement, and you give us all permissions we need to do so."
Use of Service or Content: *Right to Use Service*	None stated.	None stated.	Dropbox "grants you a limited, nonexclusive, nontransferable, revocable license to use the Software, solely to access the Services." No reverse engineering.	None stated.

Table 4. (*Continued*)

Use of Service or Content: Collection of Personal Information	Collection of location data is the default. Apple collects personal information as well as technical or diagnostic information regarding the user's Apple devices. The privacy policy is a separate policy and is not incorporated into this agreement.	"will not monitor, edit, or disclose any information regard- ing you or your account, including any Data, without your prior permission except in accordance with this Agree-ment." A privacy policy is incorporated into the terms of the Agreement but the terms of it may change. Open Drive collects registration and profile information, payment information, PC, IP address and related information, and cookies. "By using our services you consent to our collection and use of your personal information as described in this Privacy Policy."	Service claims not share personal information, but it can collect it ("To be clear, aside from the rare exceptions we identify in our Privacy Policy, no matter how the Services change, we won't share your content with others...") Of course the exceptions are in a separate document not made a part of this license.	"For example, this information may include the device type, mobile network connectivity, location of the device, information about when the Software is launched, individual session lengths for use of the Service, content used through the Service, or occurrences of technical errors."

6   Conclusion

The review and comparison of the four cloud computing services TOS reveal a number of onerous or otherwise problematic provisions. In terms of legal risk, TOS that require a user to indemnify the service for all harms such as iCloud, OpenDrive and Amazon Cloud Drive are most dangerous while at the same time providers make few if any legal promises (warranties) regarding the service availability or functionality. From a sense of user functionality a cloud provider with the fewest number of content restrictions is desirable. Dropbox appears to have the least number of content restrictions. Users of any of the four cloud TOS agreements reviewed could face termination and/or suspension for non-compliance with the TOS. Only Dropbox will attempt but not promise to provide notice of suspension or termination. Overall and as discussed above and presented in Table 4 (Comparison and Summary of Cloud Computing TOS) below, Dropbox appears the most even-handed. Hopefully this discussion provides users with an awareness of the range of issues that cloud computing EULAs or TOS can contain. While it may not be possible to negotiate for better terms, users can at least assess their comfort level with a particular service and select the least offensive option, at least in terms of the TOS. It may also be that this discussion may propel social forces to pressure cloud providers to make changes as well. Awareness is the first step towards change. While these licenses are not negotiable, general public sentiment and outcry has in the past promoted change especially in the social network arena and such mobilization or groundswell may do so here. Short of the ability to alter the TOS provided in cloud computing agreements this discussion can help users to make better decisions as more information regarding the impact or particular provisions is known.

References

1. Register.com, Inc. v. Verio, Inc., 356 F.3d 393, 430 (2d. Cir. 2004), http://scholar.google.com/scholar_case?case=16484899716954801105&q=356+F.3d+393&hl=en&as_sdt=6,50
2. Douglas v. Talk America, Inc., 495 F.3d 1062 (9th Cir. 2007), cert. denied 552 U.S. 1242 (2008), http://scholar.google.com/scholar_case?case=2000111622584998103&q=495+F.3d+1062+&hl=en&as_sdt=6,50
3. Douglas v. Talk America, Inc., 495 F.3d 1062, 1065 (9th Cir. 2007), cert. denied 552 U.S. 1242 (2008)
4. Douglas v. Talk America, Inc., 495 F.3d 1062, 1065 (9th Cir. 2007), cert. denied 552 U.S. 1242 (2008)
5. Douglas v. Talk America, Inc., 495 F.3d 1062, 1066, n. 1 (9th Cir. 2007), cert. denied 552 U.S. 1242 (2008)
6. Noah v. America Online, Inc., 261 F.Supp.2d 532 (E.D. Va. 2003) affirmed 2004 WL 602711 (4th Cir.) (unpublished), http://scholar.google.com/scholar_case?case=15686646675110928460&qNoah+v.+America+Online,+Inc.,+&hl=en&as_sdt=6,50
7. Noah v. America Online, Inc., 261 F.Supp.2d 532, 534 (E.D. Va. 2003), affirmed 2004 WL 602711 (4th Cir.) (unpublished)
8. Noah v. America Online, Inc., 261 F.Supp.2d 532, 540 (E.D. Va. 2003), affirmed 2004 WL 602711 (4th Cir.) (unpublished)
9. Noah v. America Online, Inc., 261 F.Supp.2d 532, 545 (E.D. Va. 2003), affirmed 2004 WL 602711 (4th Cir.) (unpublished)
10. Martinez v. Metabolife Intern., Inc., 6 Cal. Rptr. 3d 494, 500 (2003), http://scholar.google.com/scholar_case?case=17508538987028676925&q=Martinez+v.+Metabolife+Intern.,+Inc.,&hl=en&as_sdt=6,50
11. Agri-Business Supply Co. v. Hodge, 447 So. 2d 769, 773 (Ala. Civ. App. 1984), http://scholar.google.com/scholar_case?case=5783574511669506156&q=Agri-Business+Supply+Co.+v.+Hodge,+447+So.+2d+769&hl=en&as_sdt=6,50
12. Garner, B.: Black's Law Dictionary, Thomson West, 9th edn., p. 502. Thomson West (2009)
13. AWS Customer Agreement. Last updated March 15, 2012 (current AWS customers: See What's Changed), http://aws.amazon.com/agreement/
14. Agence France Presse v. Morel, 934 F.Supp.2d 547 (S.D.N.Y. 2013), http://scholar.google.com/scholar_case?case=13226630860983262203&q=Agence+France+Presse+v.+Morel,+2013+WL+146035+&hl=en&as_sdt=6,50

15. Sony Computer Entertainment, Inc. v. Connectix Corp., 203 F.3d 596, 609 (9th Cir. 2000), `http://scholar.google.com/scholar_case?case=7166769136737271634&q=Sony+Computer+Entertainment,+Inc.+v.+Connectix+Corp.,+203+F.3d+59&hl=en&as_sdt=6,50`

16. Sega Enterprises Ltd. v. Accolade, Inc., 977 F.2d 1510, 1514 (9th Cir. 1992), `http://scholar.google.com/scholar_case?case=12221231553971530035&q=Sega+Enterprises+Ltd.+v.+Accolade,+Inc.,+977+F.2d+1510&hl=en&as_sdt=6,50`

17. Atari Games Corp. v. Nintendo of America, Inc. Sega Enterprises Ltd. v. Accolade, Inc., 977 F.2d 1510., 975 F.2d 832 (Fed. Cir 1992), `http://scholar.google.com/scholar_case?case=12221231553971530035&q=+1514+%289th+Cir.+1992%29.+17.+Atari+Games+Corp.+v.+Ninten&hl=en&as_sdt=6,50`

18. Exemption to Prohibition on Circumvention of Copyright Protection Systems for Access Control Technologies, 75 Federal Register 43825, 43829 (2010), `http://www.google.com/url?sa=t&rct=j&q=&esrc=s&source=web&cd=1&ved=0CCYQFjAA&url=http%3A%2F%2Fwww.copyright.gov%2Ffedreg%2F2010%2F75fr43825.pdf&ei=de7rUsioFMTB2wWwiYCgBg&usg=AFQjCNF0f7irwyYafuJ6FjTkFNR-ovSRsw&bvm=bv.60444564,d.b2I.`

19. Kirtsaeng v. John Wiley & Sons, Inc., 2013 WL 1104736, `http://scholar.google.com/scholar_case?case=15712401143530412161&q=Kirtsaeng+v.+John+Wiley+%26+Sons,+Inc.,+2013+WL+1104736.&hl=en&as_sdt=6,50`

20. Capital Records, LLC v. ReDIGI Inc., 934 F. Supp. 2d 640, 655 (S.D.N.Y. 2013) (emphasis added), `http://scholar.google.com/scholar_case?case=1198724326272838457&q=Capitol+Records+v.+ReDIGI+&hl=en&as_sdt=6,50`

21. Comb v. PayPal, Inc., 218 F. Supp. 2d 1165, 1172 (N.D. Cal. 2002), `http://scholar.google.com/scholar_case?case=15174879769896251427&q=Comb+v.+PayPal,+Inc.,+218+F.+Supp.+2d+1165&hl=en&as_sdt=6,50`, citing Blake v. Ecker, 113 Cal. Rptr. 2d 422 (2001)

22. Garner, B.: Black's Law Dictionary, 9th edn. Thomson West (2009)

23. AT&T Mobility LLC v. Concepcion, 131 S.Ct. 1740 (2011), `http://scholar.google.com/scholar_case?case=17088816341526709934&q=AT%26T+Mobility+LLC+v.+Concepcion,+131+S.Ct.+1740+%282011%29.+&hl=en&as_sdt=6,50`

24. Restatement (Second) of Contracts § 208 (Unconscionable Contract or Term), comment e, Unconscionable terms. American Law Institute (1981)

Evaluation of Information Security Approaches:
A Defense Industry Organization Case

Tolga Çakmak and Şahika Eroğlu

Hacettepe University, Department of Information Management, Ankara, Turkey
{tcakmak,sahikaeroglu}@hacettepe.edu.tr

Abstract. Information security systems are important to ensure business continuity and protect organizations against potential risks. In this context organizations have to analyze their information system processes and they should develop their information systems according to results of the analysis. This paper aims to evaluate the current information security approaches in a defense industry organization in Turkey. The case of the assessment demonstrates information security standards and approaches and reflects the importance of information security implementation within the organizations. In order to achieve research objectives and aims, Information Security Assessment Tool for State Agencies (an information security assessment tool) was chosen as the research instrument for this study. The results obtained from the assessment tool revealed that major applications were implemented by the defense industry organization. According to the assessments, the study recommends that education and training programs and policies should be developed, and that interoperability of information security functions should be provided in the defense industry.

Keywords: Information security, knowledge management, information security assessment.

1   Introduction

Organizations are one of the most efficient factors for the development of communities. They generally interact with their internal and external environments. As a result of this interaction, they can create not only services or a particular product required by a target group, but also create continual information and information resources, especially in electronic environments. In this respect, it would not be wrong to say that knowledge management is a key point for organizational development with the convergence of new technologies. Besides, knowledge management provides management with information created for organizational goals, promotes organizational effectiveness and productivity, and competitive advantage.

Advancements in Internet and web technologies, new perspectives for competitive advantage and changes in administrative approaches increase the importance of knowledge management for organizations. Especially since the 1990's with the use of information systems in the modern sense, knowledge management and security issues

J.N. Gathegi et al. (Eds.): IMCW 2013, CCIS 423, pp. 112–122, 2014.

have become a vital factor for organizational development and competitive advantage in a global world. Many standards, policies, regulations, information security assessment methodologies and assessment tools have been developed for organizations. In this respect, organizations can implement information security approaches according to standards and revise their information security approaches in accordance with assessment tools, and they can also take countermeasures against determined risks as well.

In the light of the information mentioned above, this study evaluates information security level of a defense industry organization where ISO 27001 Information Security Standard has been fully implemented, as well as the information security approaches mainly used due to the nature of the organization.

2   Information Security and Developments in Turkey

Information security is one of the most important components for many organizations who achieve their organizational goals via information technologies and information systems. Blackley, McDernott and Geer [1] express that the emergence of new risks dealing with technological developments has a huge effect on organizational approaches about information security. They also indicate that risk assessments for information systems should be carried out by organizations. As many researchers, governmental organizations and their reports have demonstrated, organizations should lead in the evaluation and assessment of their own information security applications, approaches and determine organizational risks.

There are many definitions of information security in the field of organizational knowledge management and library and information science. One of these definitions emphasized that "information security is collective efforts that are made for security of information processing, protection for unauthorized access, long term preservation, migration, emulation and storage of data/information in electronic environments" [2]. Furthermore, it can be inferred that information security is not only a term about technology but it is also about organizational identity. Studies on this topic asserted that information security is important for all work processes such as creation, processing and storage of information as well as in information systems and information systems [3], [4].

The term information security was mentioned and described in Turkey for the first time in 2005 with the publication of "e-Transformation Turkey Project Principles of Interoperability Guide" [5]. The Guide identifies the main aims of information security as protection of information processed via the information life cycle (in capture, creation, usage, storage, transmission and destruction phases) within the organization and providing the privacy, integrity and accessibility of information transmitted between organizations. Security and privacy of personal information was also considered to be one of the main themes in "Information Society Strategy Action Plan (2006-2010)" that was published by the Ministry of Development. Some important points covered in the plan are listed below:

- Requirement for establishment of Information Systems Disaster Recovery Management Center,
- Preservation of information related to national security in electronic environments,
- Regulations about legal infrastructure for development of information security systems [6].

Some research on the information security approaches were also conducted in Turkey by private companies. One research (Ernst & Young Company) found that 73% of organizations make investments for information security and 50% of organizations use information security standards, while 30% of organizations do not have a connection between their risk management and information security units. Research results also revealed that information security is perceived as a technological issue by Turkish companies [7].

3   Research Design

In light of the increasing importance of information security approaches in organizations, this study focused on identifying the information security approaches of a defense industry organization in Turkey. Case study methodology was used to achieve the research objectives. As quoted from Thomas [8], case study methodology is "analyses of persons, events, decisions, periods, projects, policies, institutions, or other systems that are studied holistically by one or more methods". In addition to Thomas's definition, Zainal [9] claims that a limited number of events, conditions and relationships of real-life phenomenon can be explored and investigated via case study methodology.

In this context, the research covered by this paper particularly demonstrates the current information security approaches and explores information security requirements in the defense industry organization according to the main objectives listed below:

- to provide an insight about information security standards and approaches that have been widely used in recent years by several organizations in Turkey,
- to provide a sample assessment for information security approaches,
- to highlight the importance of information security implementation within the organizations.

The study research questions that seek to determine the information security approaches within the defense industry organization are:

- What is the level of defense industry organization according to information security assessment?
- Which information security components should be developed in the defense industry organization?
- Which information security components are the strongest points of defense industry organization?

4   Data Collection and Research Instrument

Information security assessment is defined by U.S. Department of Commerce, National Standards and Technology (NIST) in 2008 in a publication entitled Technical Guide to Information Security Testing and Assessment [10]. NIST defines Information Security Assessment as: "the process of determining how effectively an entity being assessed (e.g., host, system, network, procedure, person - known as the assessment object) meets specific security objectives". NIST also guides organizations in their information security assessments by providing descriptions of the information security assessment methods. In this regard, three assessment methods -testing, examining and interviewing- can be used for information security assessments according to NIST [10]. In this respect, examining, which is defined by NIST as: "the process of checking, inspecting, reviewing, observing, studying, or analyzing one or more assessment objects to facilitate understanding, achieve clarification, or obtain evidence" and interviewing methods were used to gather data about information security approaches in the defense industry organization.

In parallel with the study's research design and objectives, data were gathered via an assessment tool and structured individual interviews with information security experts who work in the defense industry organization. Also, in line with the research objectives, legal regulations, assessment tools, and information security standards were reviewed. As a result of the reviews, Information Security Assessment Tool for State Agencies, derived from Information Security Governance Assessment Tool for Higher Education, which was developed by EDUCAUSE in 2004 to support U.S. National Cyber Security Partnership Corporate Governance Task Force Information Security Government recommendations, was chosen for analysis.

Information Security Assessment Tool for State Agencies was developed with the aim of evaluation of the people, process, and technology components of cyber security [11]. This tool is also viewed as a pointer for organizations in terms of the maturity of their information security program. The sections in this tool can be divided into two main parts consisting of reliance of information technology and the maturity of information security governance.

The assessment tool consists of five sections and a scoring tool. Each section has multiple choice and/or Likert scale questions (0 – Not implemented, 4 – Fully implemented). The quantitative data presented in the study were gathered via additional information areas that are provided by the assessment tool for every question. The sections of the assessment tool are organizational reliance on IT, risk management, people, processes and technology. Plus, the scoring tool section of the tool provides total score of each section and reflects organizations' general level. In this respect results obtained from the scoring tool were evaluated under the general overview title according to percentage values.

5   Data Analysis

Qualitative and quantitative findings obtained via the assessment tool were analyzed according to scoring section of the tool. The data that were gathered via the tool created a score, which demonstrates information security, level of the organization in terms of the organizational reliance on information technology, people, risk management, processes and technology. Scores obtained in these sections were reported and evaluated to reflect current situation and needs of defense industry organization.

6   Results

In this section of the study, results obtained from the assessment tool, Information Security Assessment Tool for State Agencies, are presented. In parallel with the research objectives, assessment tool provides overall assessment and considers current situation, requirements and improvements for the defense industry organization. In this context, assessment tool indicates the results of main components of information security like organizational reliance on IT, risk management, people, processes, technology and general overview.

6.1   Organizational Reliance on IT

In the beginning of the assessment, general structure of the test-bed and organizational reliance on IT of the defense industry organization were identified by the multiple choice and Likert scale questions. According to results, annual budget of the organization (between $100 million to $1 billion) is in medium level. Results also reflect that the defense industry organization is at a very low level with its number of employees (less than 500 employees).

Organizational reliance on IT and general characteristics of the test-bed were investigated via 11 Likert scale and 2 multiple-choice questions. According to the answers given to this part of the tool, the defense industry organization is at high level in terms of dependence upon information technology systems and the Internet to offer services to customers, outreach programs, conduct research, and support services. Assessment regarding the value of the organization's intellectual property stored and transmitted in electronic form places it at the medium level. Information security experts thought the impact of major system downtime on operations is in medium level for the organization as well.

According to the results, the degree of change within the organization, impact on the organization's operations from an Internet outage, dependency on multi-site operations, and plans for multi-site operations (i.e. outsourced business functions, multiple locations and new collaborations) are at a low level. Information security experts also noted that the organization is at a very low level in terms of preparation for potential impact to national or critical infrastructure in case of outage, interruption, or compromise to systems. It is also noted that sensitivity of stakeholders and customers to security and privacy, and extent of operations dependent upon third parties, are at a high level. Furthermore, it was determined that the organization's level of regulation regarding security and privacy is at mid-level.

Lastly, potential impacts on reputation of security incidents (i.e. negative press and political pressure) are in low level for the organization according to information security experts. It is also stated that the organization has low business programs in a politically sensitive area that may make it a target of a violent physical or cyber-attack from any groups.

6.2   Risk Management

Information security experts were asked to describe risk management approaches of the organization via nine Likert scale questions provided by the second part of the assessment tool. Risk management approaches are one of the main functions of the organizations in the defense industry. Experts stated that the whole of the risk management metrics are fully implemented. These risk management metrics are as follows:

- Information security and privacy program were fully documented,
- Risk assessments to identify key objectives that need to be supported by the information security and privacy program were conducted within the last two years,
- Critical assets and relevant business functions were fully identified,
- Information security threats and vulnerabilities associated with each of the critical assets and functions were fully identified,
- Costs and cost analysis for the loss of each critical asset or function were carried out,
- A written information security strategy that seeks to cost-effectively measure risk and specify actions to manage risk at an acceptable level with minimal business disruptions was developed,
- Information security strategy of the organization fully includes plans that seek to cost effectively reduce the risks to acceptable level,
- Information security strategy of the organization is reviewed and updated at least annually or more frequently when significant business changes require it,
- Processes to monitor legislation or regulations and determine their applicability to the organization were fully implemented.

6.3   People

Another section of the assessment tool within the scope of information security approaches is assessment of people in the organization. In this regard, the analyses involve the answers given to questions about responsibilities, management, information security functions, and education and training program. The results obtained from the analyses about this part of the assessment tool are displayed at Fig. 1.

According to the results in Fig. 1, the organization meets the most of the requirements about responsibilities (90%), management (94%) and information security functions (88%). However, it was found that only half of the education and training program requirements can be met with existing information security approaches of the organization.

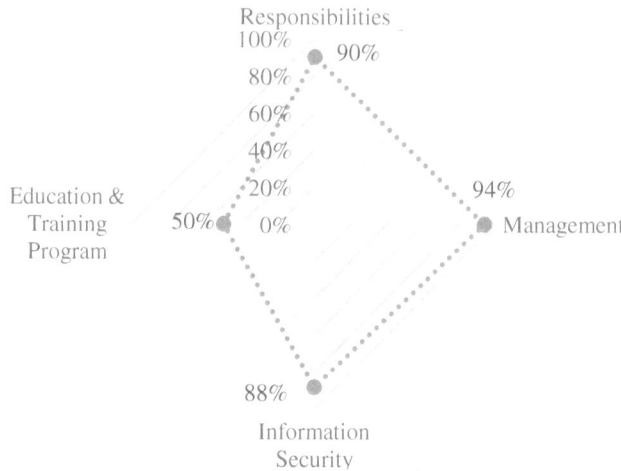

Fig. 1. Information security approaches in terms of people in defense industry organization

According to the results demonstrated in Fig. 1, Information security experts stated that only some units have employees for liaising with business units to identify any new security requirements based on changes to the operations. It is also indicated that most of the business unit managers and senior managers have specific programs in place to comply with information security and privacy policies and standards. Furthermore, results reflect that most of the information security functions were actively engaged with other critical functions such as IT, Human Resources, etc. On the other hand, education and training program requirements about information security and privacy issues were only partially implemented by the organization.

6.4   Processes

Analyses on information security processes were considered under five titles by the assessment tool. These titles are security technology strategy, policy development and enforcement, information security and procedures, physical security, and security program administration. In this context, the ratings related to the information security processes in the defense industry organization are displayed in Fig. 2.

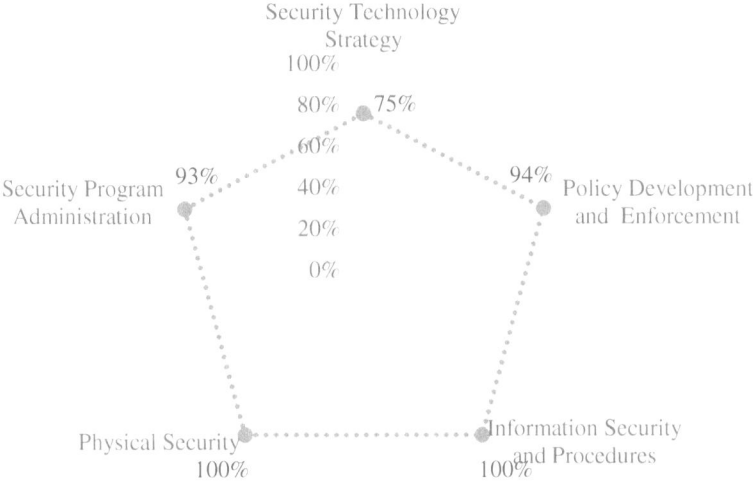

Fig. 2. Information security processes in defense industry organization

As can be seen in Fig. 2, the organization has fully implemented processes about information security and procedures, and physical security processes. On the other hand, existing processes can only meet 75% of the requirements regarding security technology strategy. It is also considered that most of the requirements regarding security program administration (93%) and policy development and enforcement (94%) are covered by the organization. The assessment tool also reveals that the organization is close to completion of following required processes in terms of security technology strategy:

- Periodical updates of the security technology strategy,
- Review of existing systems,
- Processes and procedures involving the security personnel in evaluating and addressing any security impacts before the purchase or introduction of new systems,
- Identification of work processes for incompatible systems in terms of information security,
- Implementation of specific, documented, security related configuration settings for all systems and applications,
- Developments for patch management strategy, policy and procedures.

Assessment tool also reflects that the periodic evaluation of information security and privacy program, and practices for each business unit is not fully implemented by the organization. However, analysis on political development and updates are close to completion in the organization.

6.5   Technology

Technology as one of the key information security components was also investigated by 17 Likert scale questions. According to information security experts of the defense industry organization, results indicate that 15 requirements are fully implemented. These requirements can be classified under the following titles:

- Protection of internet-accessible servers by more than one security layer,
- Controls between the layers of end-tier systems,
- Scanning of organization's networks, systems and applications in regular time intervals,
- Monitoring networks, systems and applications for unauthorized access or anomalous behavior,
- Log records of security-related activities such as hardware and software configuration, changes and access attempts,
- Enforcement processes for password change management.

Beyond these requirements, confidential, personal or sensitive data are not encrypted and associated encryption keys are not properly protected by the organization. There is not an authentication system in place that applies higher levels of authentication to protect resources with higher levels of sensitivity.

6.6   General Overview

Apart from the specific results about essential components of information security, a general overview for the whole organization was also provided by the assessment tool in order to present whole capabilities and requirements. In this context, general overview for the information security approaches of the defense industry organization is demonstrated in Fig. 3.

As can be seen in Fig. 3, risk management approaches and processes are prominent components (respectively with the rates of 100% and 93%) for the organization. Technology is the third component with the rate of 88% while people is fourth (77%). On the other hand organizational reliance on IT is quite low because of the defense industry's nature and some security measures applied by the organization.

In the light of the assessments, the scoring section of the assessment tool indicates that organizational reliance on IT of the defense industry organization is at the medium level and overall assessment shows that organization is at a good level with 300 points calculated, based on the responses for each section of the assessment tool.

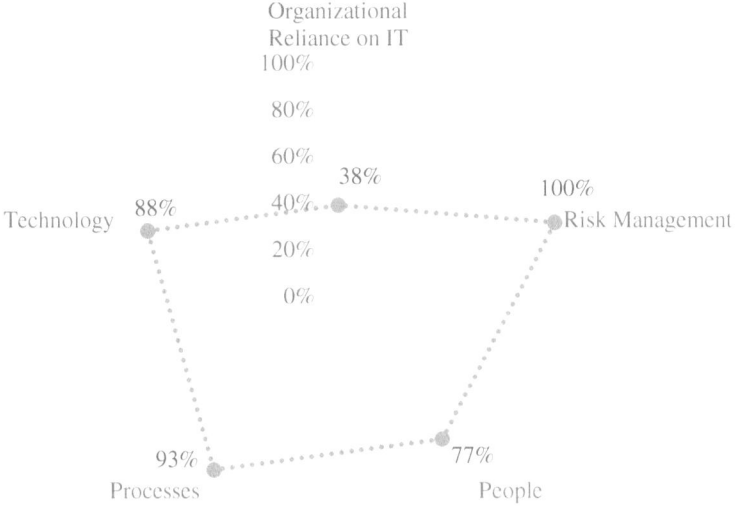

Fig. 3. General overview

7   Conclusion and Recommendations

Information security is an important factor for all types of organizations. Moreover, the defense industry is one of the most important sectors for risk and information security management in changing technological conditions. Implementation and adaptation of the information security standards and policies are essential factors for organizations in the defense industry. Additionally, it can be said that measurements and analysis that reflect current situations are important, as are utility factors. In this context, the results generated from the tool provided a detailed insight for information security approaches of the defense industry organization in terms of IT reliance, people, processes, risk management and technology.

The results of our study with respect to information security applications show that major applications were implemented by the defense industry organization. Furthermore, organizational reliance on IT for the defense industry organization is in the low level range by reason of security measures. Additionally results reflect that the defense industry organization is among the medium scaled companies and its approaches are in the good level range. On the other hand the organization has a stronger profile in terms of risk management and technology factors of information security.

In light of the results of this study, it can be suggested that attempts and some improvements should be made to increase effectiveness of information security approaches. These attempts can be listed as follows:

- Personnel requirements should be met for liaising with business units to identify any new security requirements based on changes to the operations.

- Policies that comply with information security policy, standards and regulations should be developed for all managers and senior managers.
- Interoperability of information security functions with other critical assets and functions should be provided to improve information security and privacy policies and applications.
- Education and training programs should be implemented for all employees.

Results about processes show that, information security, privacy programs and performance metrics should be completely evaluated and tested for each business unit. Additionally, policy development and update analysis should be entirety implemented.

Technological approaches are another stronger side of the defense industry organization. Assessments reflect that an authentication system that can be applied to higher levels of authentication to protect resources should be implemented. Data encryptions and associated encryption keys should be protected via new information security approaches as well.

References

1. Blackley, B., McDermott, E., Geer, D.: Information Security is Information Risk Management. In: Proceedings of the 2001 Workshop on New Security Paradigms, pp. 97–104. ACM, New York (2001)
2. Canbek, G., Sağıroğlu, Ş.: Bilgi, Bilgi Güvenliği ve Süreçleri Üzerine Bir İnceleme [An Evaluation on Information, Information Security and Processes]. Politeknik Dergisi 9(3), 165–174 (2006)
3. Doğantimur, F.: ISO 27001 Çerçevesinde Kurumsal Bilgi Güvenliği [Organizational Information Security within the Framework of ISO 27001]. Unpublished thesis of professional competence, Ministry of Finance (2009)
4. Vural, Y., Sağıroğlu, Ş.: Kurumsal Bilgi Güvenliği ve Standartları Üzerine bir İnceleme [A Review on Organizational Information Security and Standards]. Gazi Üniversitesi Mühendislik ve Mimarlık Fakültesi Dergisi 23(2), 507–522 (2008)
5. DPT: e-Dönüşüm Türkiye Projesi Birlikte Çalışabilirlik Esasları Rehberi [e-Transformation Turkey Project Principles of Interoperability Guide]. Devlet Planlama Teşkilatı, Ankara (2005)
6. DPT: Bilgi Toplumu Stratejisi Eylem Planı (2006- 2010) [Information Society Strategy Action Plan (2006- 2010)]. Devlet Planlama Teşkilatı, Ankara (2006)
7. Bilisim 2023 Derneği, http://bilisim2023.org/index.php?option=com_content&view=article&id=189:tuerkyede-blg-guevenl-yatirimlari-artiyor&catid=7:goerueler&Itemid=18
8. Thomas, G.: A Typology for the Case Study in Social Science Following a Review of Definition, Discourse and Structure. Qualitative Inquiry 17(6), 511–521 (2011)
9. Zainal, Z.: Case Study as a Research Method. Jurnal Kemanusiaan Bil 9, 1–5 (2007)
10. Scarfone, K., Souppaya, M., Cody, A., Orebaugh, A.: Technical Guide to Information Security Testing and Assessment: Recommendations of the National Institute of Standards and Technology. U.S. Department of Commerce, Gaithersburg (2008)
11. Risk Assessment Toolkit, http://www.cio.ca.gov/OIS/government/risk/toolkit.asp

Information-Seeking Behavior of Undergraduate, Graduate, and Doctoral Students: A Survey of Istanbul University, Turkey

Hülya Dilek-Kayaoglu

Istanbul University, Faculty of Letters, Department of Information Management
34400 Eminonu, Istanbul, Turkey
dilekkayaoglu@gmail.com

Abstract. The main purpose of this study is to examine the research habits of undergraduate, graduate, and doctoral students at Istanbul University. Specifically, the study tries to develop a deeper understanding of the changing nature of participants' general research processes and their information-seeking behavioral patterns. Moreover, the study investigates whether academic level and discipline influence participants' information-seeking behavior. Based on survey findings, the author makes recommendations for improving both students' information literacy levels and library services to better meet the needs of users.

Keywords: Information-seeking behavior, information literacy skills, Turkey.

1   Introduction

The term "information-seeking behavior" has been used in professional literature since the mid-twentieth century. Today, this subject investigates the ways people seek and use information, with library and information science operating as a sub-discipline. This field has become increasingly important in light of profound changes in information and communication technologies, especially in the last ten years, as so-called "millennial" students have entered higher education.

Over the past several years, many important studies have discussed students' changing use of digital content. Of particular note is the work done by Joint Information System Committee (JISC) [1] in the United Kingdom, and Project Information Literacy [2] out of the University of Washington's Information School. According to the latter study, for many of today's undergraduates, the idea of being able to conduct an exhaustive search is inconceivable; to them, information seems to be as limitless as the universe [3]. As research is one of the most difficult challenges facing students in the digital age, knowledge of users' information needs and information-seeking behavior are vital for developing strategies and practices to support students undertaking and investigating the nature of research.

The main purpose of this study is to examine the research habits of undergraduates and postgraduates at Istanbul University. Specifically, the study tries to develop a

J.N. Gathegi et al. (Eds.): IMCW 2013, CCIS 423, pp. 123–136, 2014.
© Springer-Verlag Berlin Heidelberg 2014

deeper understanding of the changing nature of participants' general research process and the patterns of their information-seeking behavior. In order to better understand how students behave when seeking information for course-related research, we posed five research questions:

- How do undergraduates and postgraduates seek and obtain information they need for course-related research?
- Who is their best resource for help or advice in the research process?
- How do they judge the quality of information resources they find?
- What techniques and routines do students use for fulfilling research assignments?
- What are the major issues they face in conducting research?

2   Background and Methodology

Istanbul University is an education, research, and service center with twenty faculties (two of which are research hospitals belonging to the Faculty of Medicine) located at eleven campuses, one conservatory, six vocational high schools, and seventeen institutes. The University offers an integrated education system extending from primary to PhD level. In order to investigate the research habits of undergraduates and postgraduates at the university, a descriptive online survey questionnaire was used. This was the preferred method for data collection due to the large size and wide geographical distribution of the sample.

The survey used 12 questions adapted from studies previously done by Head and Eisenberg [3], [4], George et al [5] and Martin [6], allowing this study to be compared with these and other related studies. Before launching the survey, its wording and functionality was pre-tested with five undergraduates who were enrolled in the Faculty of Letters. Based on this feedback, some survey questions were re-worded and two of them were clarified. The final questionnaire with closed, multiple choice questions was published on the university's website on June 15, 2013.

The analyzed sample consisted of (N= 87,044) [7] students; 458 replies were received, but 9 of those were blank. Consequently, the self-selected sample of the survey consisted of 449 students (n= 449). A sample size of 449 that gives a statistical accuracy of + or - 5% with 96% confidence can be regarded as reasonable. The collected data were coded and analyzed by a statistician using SPSS version 11.5 for Windows. The data were then tabulated using tables and percentages. The chi-square test was used to compare categorical values. In order to establish the relationship between two variables, the Pearson correlation test was used, with an accepted level of significance of $p \leq 0.05$ (p= level of significance).

In particular, the survey asked respondents to answer questions about: (i) general research habits, (ii) resources they use for class projects, (iii) which resource they preferred to use (library or the Internet) (iv) people whom they ask for help and advice during the research process, (v) criteria they use for evaluating web resources, (vi) research styles, routines and techniques they use, and (vii) the major issues they experience in conducting research.

3   Results

The sample was nearly equally divided between male and female respondents. Among the 449 users who responded to the survey, 51.2% were female and 47.9% were male. 1% of the respondents declined to state their sexual orientation or skipped the question. Many of the respondents (61%) were aged 23 or over, followed by those aged between 18 and 22 years (38.8%). Only one student under the age of 18 answered the questionnaire. With regard to respondents' current academic level, the majority of the respondents were undergraduates (58%) and the rest were postgraduates (42%). Figure 1 details students' academic level. The majority of respondents were master's students (27.4%), followed by third year undergraduates (26.3%), doctoral students (15.4%), fourth year undergraduates (11.6%), and second year undergraduates (11.4%). Sixth grade students (interns) of the Faculty of Medicine (4.4%) and first year students (3.6%) are least represented in this survey. Freshman students' reluctance to answer the questionnaire is understandable given their limited course-research experience.

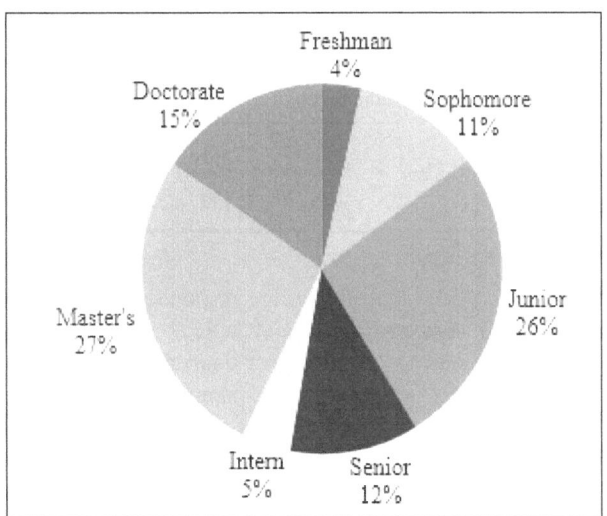

Fig. 1. Academic level of students

Regarding area of study, regardless of major, it was observed that most of the respondents were from the social sciences (47.9%), followed by the natural sciences with 20.5%, humanities with 17.6%, and health sciences with 13.6%. These results reflect the statistical ratio of graduates to postgraduates, as well as that of social science students to humanities students, in the general student population as reported by the university [7].

3.1   Student Research Habits

In order to understand the respondents' research habits, three specific statements were proposed, and the respondents' agreement or disagreement was recorded. These statements were as follows:

- "I enjoy doing research";
- "I am required to write research papers for my classes"; and
- "I generally feel prepared to conduct the required research."

Table 1. Research habits of students

I enjoy doing research					
Strongly Agree	Agree	Neither Agree Nor Disagree	Disagree	Strongly Disagree	Declined to State
51%, n=229	38.1%, n=171	7.1%, n=32	2.2%,n=10	1.3%, n=6	0.2%, n=1
I am required to write research papers for my classes					
Strongly Agree	Agree	Neither Agree Nor Disagree	Disagree	Strongly Disagree	Declined to State
35.9%, n=161	38.8%, n=174	11.4%, n=51	6%, n=27	5.8%,n=26	2.2%,n=10
I generally feel prepared to conduct the required research					
Strongly Agree	Agree	Neither Agree Nor Disagree	Disagree	Strongly Disagree	Declined to State
18.7%, n=84	41.6%, n=187	26.1%, n=117	10%, n=45	2%, n=9	1.6%, n=7

As revealed in Table 1, the majority of the respondents stated that they enjoyed doing research (combined "agree strongly" and "agree" responses totaled 89.1%), and that they had to write a research paper for their courses (74.7%). Almost 60% of the respondents agreed or strongly agreed with the statement, "I generally feel prepared to conduct the required research", while 26.1% of respondents were neutral, and 12% disagreed or strongly disagreed. Skipped or declined questions could also be interpreted as disagreement. When this statement was analyzed by academic level, a statistically significant inverse relationship was observed between "feeling prepared to conduct the research" and the academic level of respondents (chi-square= 60,135, degrees of freedom: 3, $p \leq 0.001$). Figure 2 shows that postgraduate respondents reported the highest level of agreement ("agree" and "agree strongly" responses) with this statement (56%), while undergraduate respondents reported the highest level of disagreement ("disagree" and "disagree strongly" responses) (90.7%). Taken together, survey data show that the majority of students surveyed are engaged in course-related research and enjoy it. However, as expected, postgraduates feel more prepared to conduct this research than undergraduates do.

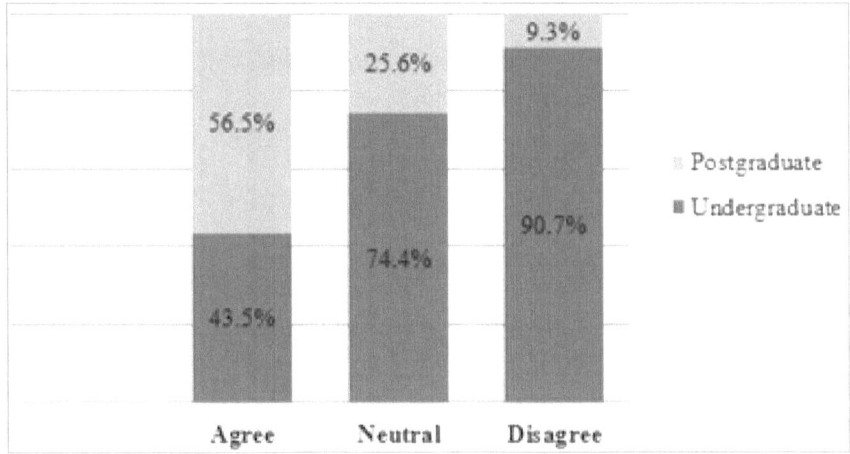

Fig. 2. "Feel prepared to conduct the required research" by academic level

3.2   Resources Used for Class Projects

To identify the types of resources students used to find information for their class projects (e.g. papers, oral presentations), respondents were asked: "when writing a typical research paper in a university class, where would you find most of your information?" Overall, results reveal that, as many librarians and educators had previously assumed, search engines (e.g. Google) were the primary choice of almost 90% of respondents for class-related research (Fig. 3). The next most popular choice was constantly available online resources (e.g. library e-resources and databases), which allow students to collect information using their computers from any location, at any time (consistent with the 2009 PIL survey). Class materials (e.g. lecture notes and textbooks) were also valued sources of information for the respondents. On the other hand, they were less likely to use library print resources than library e-resources, and consulted Wikipedia to a lesser extent than search engines, library e-resources and databases, class material and library print resources. Taken together, these data suggest that students strongly preferred research resources that were quickly and easily accessible.

The preference for search engines over library print resources, however, was not limited to inexperienced undergraduate students. When cross-tabulating the frequency of search engine use according to academic level and discipline, only discipline was statistically significantly associated with frequency of use (chi-square= 24.632, degrees of freedom: 12, $p \leq 0.017$). Figure 4 shows that the percentage of respondents who frequently used search engines was evenly distributed among all disciplines. However, the majority of frequent e-journal users (combined "always" and "often" responses) were humanities students (48.1%), followed by health sciences with 47.5%, natural sciences with 46.7%, and social sciences with 39.1%. On the other hand, respondents who rarely used search engines (combined "rarely" and "never" responses) were primarily humanities students (30.4%), natural sciences (29.3%), social sciences (28.4%), and health sciences (14.8%).

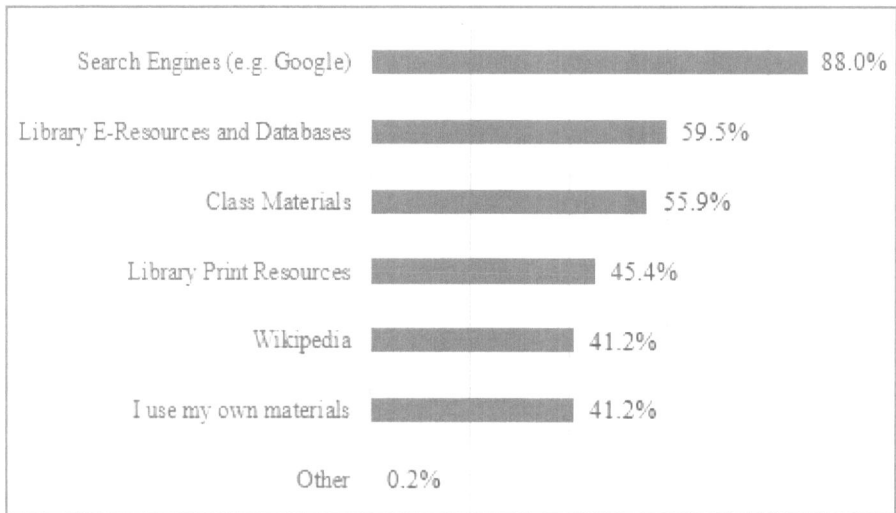

Fig. 3. Sources used for course-related research. Results are ranked from most frequent to least frequent resources students used for class-related research. Responses of "almost always", and "often" have been combined.

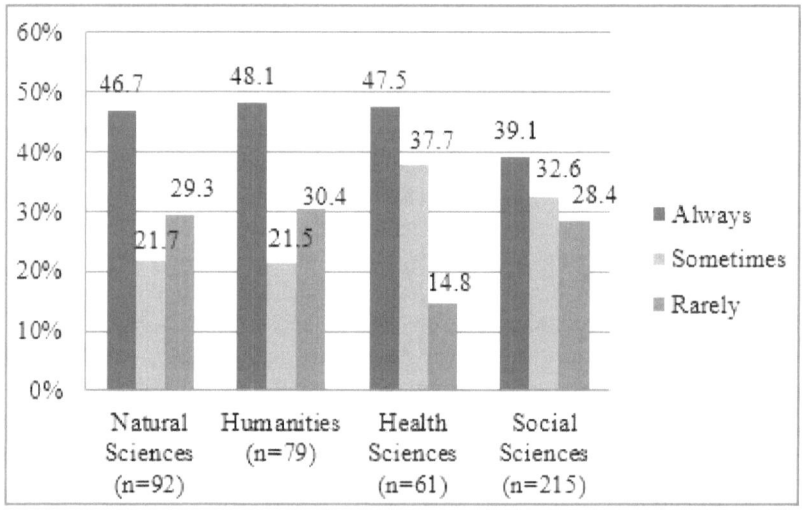

Fig. 4. Use of search engines for course - related research by discipline. Responses of ("almost always" and "often") and ("rare" and "never") have been combined

3.3   Resource Preference: Library vs. Internet

As revealed above in Figure 3, respondents used Google and other search engines more frequently than they used university library resources for their class projects. This finding raises the question: what drives this preference? In order to answer this question, several specific statements were provided, and respondents' agreement and disagreement were recorded. As can be seen in Table 2, most of the respondents (43.2%) chose their preferred resource based on convenience of access, even if it was not the best resource for their topic. Additionally, they preferred online resources (WWW) to the library's print (70.6%) and electronic resources (53.5%). Dishearteningly, the majority of respondents reported that they needed help using libraries' print or e-resources and services. Responses also revealed that students are not quite familiar with library services and are under confident about using library resources. As a whole, these findings are consistent with Figure 3, and suggest that convenience may be the key to resource preference.

Table 2. Preferences for resource library or WWW

I would use a source because it is convenient to use even though it is not the best source on my topic.					
Strongly Agree	Agree	Neither Agree Nor Disagree	Disagree	Strongly Disagree	Declined to State
14.5%, n=65	28.7%,n=129	29%, n=130	22%, n=99	5.3%, n=24	0.4%, n=2

I am more comfortable using the WWW than the library's resources.					
Strongly Agree	Agree	Neither Agree Nor Disagree	Disagree	Strongly Disagree	Declined to State
29.8%, n=134	40.8%,n=183	17.1%, n=77	8%, n=36	2.4%, n=11	1.8%, n=8

I am more comfortable using the WWW than the library's e-resources.					
Strongly Agree	Agree	Neither Agree Nor Disagree	Disagree	Strongly Disagree	Declined to State
21.2%, n=95	32.3%,n=145	25.4%, n=114	14.7%, n=66	3.10%, n=14	3.3%,n=15

I need help for using libraries' print or e-resources and services					
Strongly Agree	Agree	Neither Agree Nor Disagree	Disagree	Strongly Disagree	Declined to State
17.4%, n=78	32.4%,n=145	23.7%, n=106	19.9%, n=89	4.5%, n=20	2.2%, n=1

3.4   Asking for Help and Advice during the Research Process

Fig. 5 reveals that academics (e.g. advisors, professors, and committee members) have the most influence on students' research processes. More than half of the students (56.8%) reported that they consulted academic staff for guidance during their research. This result was consistent across the disciplines (66% in natural sciences, 61% in humanities, 55% in social sciences, and 44.3% in health sciences), but varied across academic levels (46.7% of undergraduates as opposed to 70.3% of postgraduates). It should be noted that there was a statistically significant inverse relationship between "asking for help or advice from academics" and academic level

of respondents (chi-square= 31.151, degrees of freedom: 3, p≤ 0.001). Of the
respondents, 70% who indicated they always or often sought help from academics
were postgraduates, whereas 22% of the respondents who indicated they rarely sought
help from academics were undergraduates.

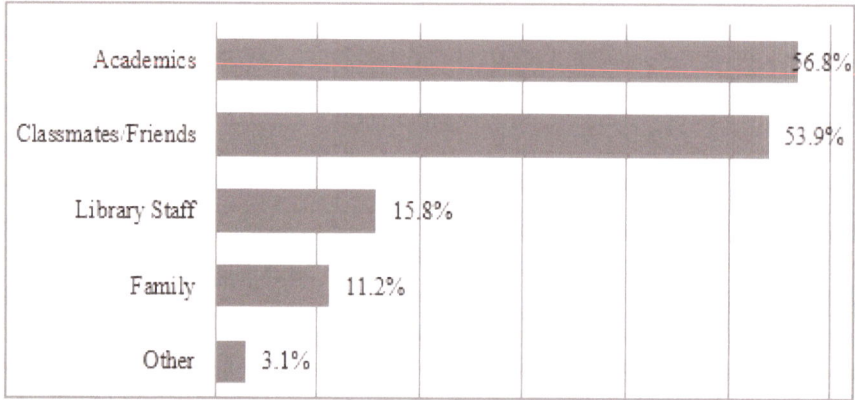

Fig. 5. Asking for help or advice. Results are ranked from most frequent to least frequent used
people that students turn to for help or advice. Responses of "almost always" and "often" have
been combined.

Asking a classmate or friend for help with their research was the second most
popular choice among respondents; as expected, undergraduates tended to favor this
method more than postgraduates did. Survey data also showed that a large amount of
respondents excluded library staff from their research process: only 16% of the
respondents answered that they frequently use librarians. On the other hand, when
these responses were organized by academic level, it was observed that graduates
were more likely to consult library staff than postgraduates were. Seeing library staff
occupying such a limited role in students' research process is, of course, quite
discouraging. It was also interesting that some respondents preferred to ask for help or
advice from a family member than from an academic or librarian.

3.5   Evaluating Web Sources

The survey findings show that respondents often evaluate web content for course-related
research (Fig. 6). When evaluating web sources in the course of their research, the
majority of respondents ranked reliability as their main criterion (96.7%), followed by
currency at 90.2%, convenience at 79.7%, and format at 67.9%. Overall, these findings
suggest that respondents consider resource reliability and timeliness to be extremely
important, but convenience and format are nearly as important. When these criteria were
analyzed by discipline and academic level, no relationship with discipline could be
determined; however, it was found that undergraduates were more likely than
postgraduates to favor convenience above other criteria.

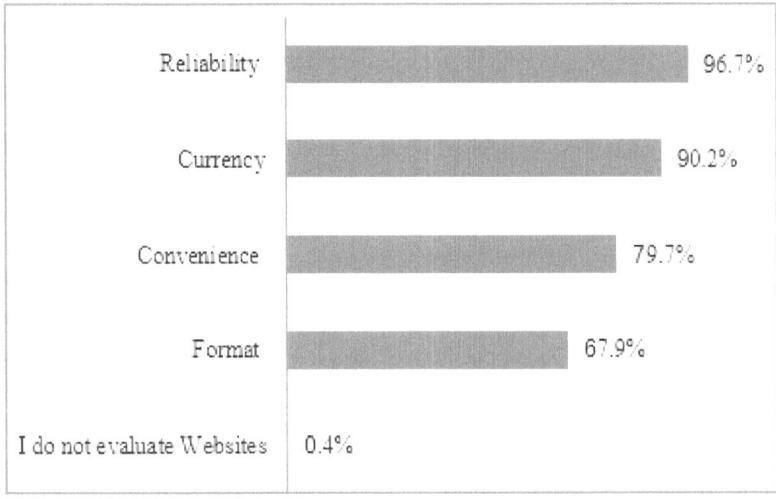

Fig. 6. Criteria for evaluating Web resources. Results are ranked from most important to least important evaluation criteria students have while evaluating the web sources. Responses of "very important" and "important" have been combined.

3.6   Research Styles and Routine Techniques

Student use different research styles -that is, practices, techniques, and approaches- to prepare research papers. Fig. 7 shows the practices and approaches used by respondents when preparing research papers, ranked by frequency of use from most to least. Most of the respondents used routines and techniques at the writing stage, such as developing an outline for guidance (71%) and creating a thesis statement (48%),

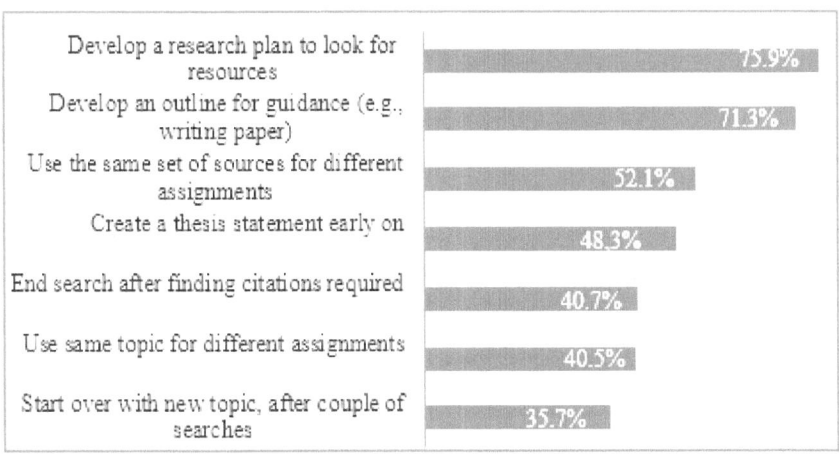

Fig. 7. Research styles

as well as at the research stage, such as planning where to look for resources (76%). They also used some time- and energy-saving routines, such as ending a search after finding the citations they required (41%), and choosing an entirely new topic if they could not find research materials in their first couple of attempts (36%). On the other hand, one particularly discouraging finding was that most students were "cheating themselves" by using the same research topic for multiple courses (41%).

3.7   Major Issues in Conducting Research

Difficulties during the entire research process, from the moment students receive the assignment until they turn in their research paper, are inevitable. In order to better understand the issues students encounter when conducting research, respondents recorded their agreement and disagreement with several statements describing common research difficulties.

Table 3 shows these statements and the students' responses. For nearly three-quarters of the respondents (73.2%), the most difficult step of the research process was starting the assignment, followed by defining a topic (62.6%), narrowing down a topic (60%), and finding web sources (57%). When these three difficulties were organized by academic level and discipline, a significant association was observed between discipline and difficulty in starting an assignment, with social science students reporting greater difficulty in starting their research than students in other disciplines. Other major barriers reported by respondents include determining a website's credibility (57%), time pressure (56%), finding articles in library research databases (47%) and finding up-to-date resources (46%). On the other hand, taking notes (41%), knowing how to cite sources (39.4%) and, writing about their findings (36.3%) were the steps with which students relatively felt themselves equipped to their research.

Table 3. Major issues in conducting research

	Agree (%)	Neither Agree Nor Disagree (%)	Disagree (%)	Declined to State (%)
Getting started is difficult	73.2	17.80	5.8	3.10
Defining a topic is difficult	62.6	20.9	14.3	2.20
Narrowing down a topic	60.2	24.7	11.8	3.30
Finding articles in research databases of the library	47.0	30.7	19.8	2.40
Finding Web sources	57.4	21.2	18.5	2.90
Determining whether a Web Site is credible or not is difficult	56.6	22.0	18.0	3.30
Finding up-to-date resources	46.1	27.4	23,9	2.70
Taking notes	29.9	26.1	41.0	3.10
Writing about what is found	41,2	19.2	36,3	3.30
Knowing how to cite resources	30.0	27.2	39.4	3.30
Time limit	55.9	21.2	19.4	3.60

4   Discussion

Previous studies have indicated that students use search engines as their main information resource [1], [3], [4], [5], [6], [8], [9], [10], [11]. This study appears to confirm this finding. Almost all respondents frequently use search engines, and undergraduates in particular tend to be more inclined to use search engines as their main source of information. The main reason students prefer search engines is because they can find information more easily and quickly than by using their library's print or electronic resources.

However, just because students can use a search engine does not necessarily mean they have the skills to find important course-related resources, evaluate them critically, and use them effectively. Therefore, this finding suggests that students are deficient in basic information literacy. They do not necessarily understand the different ways in which the Internet affects their learning and research habits. Students' reported difficulties using library resources and services could also be evidence of this deficiency. On the other hand, search engines are an undeniable mainstay of modern information gathering; therefore, rather than disregarding their value, students must concern themselves with how to make the best use of search engines (in line with JISC, 2009) [1].

In contrast to some previous studies, this study found that students actually do use university libraries. While the majority of the students used search engines as their primary method of gathering information, most of the students also included the library in their research process, particularly the library's online resources. That said, this study also found that most students need help using library services and resources, both print and electronic. This finding is easily understandable in a local context: in Turkey, students are not taught basic information literacy before they get to university. While Istanbul University's Central Library conducts a one-off annual freshman orientation, this is insufficient to foster true information literacy; therefore, it is unfair to expect students to engage with library services and resources when they first enroll at university. The Central Library can provide library instruction throughout the term, inform students of the services and resources available to them, and teach them how to use them. In this regard, there is a need for a more systemic approach to university-wide information literacy in which all stakeholders - academics, librarians, and administrators- have responsibility.

Consistent with previous research students mostly consider academics as sources for help or advice for their course-related research [4], [5]. In addition, postgraduates are more inclined to ask for help from academics than undergraduates are. Most of the students also value their friends as sources of information and assistance and, as expected, undergraduates use their classmates or friends for information more than postgraduates do. It is understandable that students see academics as the most influential people in the research process; as knowledgeable people, academics offer guidance and direction on how best to cope with the complexity of the research process. This places them in a key position to affect students' information behavior. Therefore, academics need to perceive course-related projects as a means of teaching students how to learn, as well as helping them develop higher-order research skills.

Although librarians are experts in finding the best research practices and resources, including new technology, it is a discouraging finding that most of the students surveyed do not consider librarians as resources when seeking help. Even though students use library resources and services, especially e-resources, they mostly prefer to exclude librarians from the research process. (The PIL study (2009) identified a similar finding in the context of web resource evaluation [4]). Additionally, it should be noted that postgraduates are less likely to consult librarians than undergraduates are. Istanbul University's library organization and employment can partially explain this finding. While the Central and faculty libraries tend to employ professional librarians, the departmental libraries (which are under functioning) tend to employ mostly non-professional librarians. Naturally, this situation causes students to develop misconceptions about the role and the value of librarians, resulting in students excluding library staff from their research. This highlights an urgent need to raise the profile of professional librarians in the student community, as well as the need for regular training and refresher courses for non-professionals. Restructuring Istanbul University's library systems should also be reconsidered.

As found in previous studies students often evaluate web resources for course-related research [4], [5]. In their evaluation, students are more likely to use criteria such as resource reliability and currency of information, although format and convenience are nearly as important to them. Though there was no observed relationship between discipline and criteria used, it was shown that undergraduate students are most likely to select the criterion of convenience when evaluating web sources for research suitability. On the other hand, although students say they evaluate web resources in general, they have trouble using evaluative criteria. For example, determining the credibility of a website or finding an article in the library's research database is difficult for the majority of students.

Although the majority of the students state that they use specific routines and techniques for conducting research, the problems they experience while researching suggest that these routines cannot always help them overcome their difficulties. For example, most students had great difficulty defining and narrowing a research topic, as well as starting the paper. It is particularly noteworthy that these first three difficulties and their order of importance are consistent with previous studies [3]. Notably, social science students seem to have more difficulty starting their assignments than other students. The Association of College and Research Libraries (ACRL) cites Bloom's Taxonomy of Educational Objectives [12] with regard to the need for recognizing different levels of thinking skills associated with teaching and learning information literacy outcomes. According to the ACRL, lower-order thinking skills are associated with standards for devising and using an effective search strategy, while higher-order thinking skills are associated with synthesizing information "to create new concepts" [13]. With these concepts in mind, our findings suggest that students need assistance with higher-order thinking skills associated with information synthesis.

5   Conclusion

The main purpose of this study was to gain a deeper understanding of how students at Istanbul University behave when seeking information for their course-related research, and whether factors such as academic level and discipline influence this behavior. An online user study was conducted to answer these questions. Although there were some variations, the findings of the survey were generally consistent with the current literature, and emphasize that information behavior tends to vary by academic level.

There is an ongoing discussion in library and information science literature that claims students lack information literacy skills and use public web resources rather than university libraries. This study seems to support these claims, showing that students strongly prefer quickly and easily accessible resources, whether they are the university library's online resources, or general Internet sources. On the other hand, this study also indicates that students need help to use the library's services and resources, as well as finding and evaluating web resources. This finding clearly shows that students need support when undertaking and understanding the nature of research.

It is of course unfair and unreasonable to expect this of university students who were not taught information literacy at secondary school. Therefore, Istanbul University's Central Library should provide library instruction throughout the term, and raise awareness among students about the services and resources that are available by working with the faculty libraries. Additionally, as mentioned in the ACRL report (2000), incorporating information literacy across curricula, in all programs and services, and throughout the administrative life of the university, requires the collaborative efforts of faculty, librarians, and administrators. Through collaborative efforts, faculty establishes the context for learning and inspires students to explore the unknown, librarians evaluate resources and provide library services and instruction, and administrators create opportunities for collaboration and provide ongoing resources to sustain information literacy initiatives.

It is also critically important to develop a national strategy and/or framework in collaboration with an authoritative body (such as the National Ministry of Education) in order to provide principles, standards, and practices that can support information literacy education in all education sectors.

The chief limitation of this study was its relatively small sample size. For this reason, these findings cannot be generalized to the broader community based on this research alone. Therefore, more in-depth research should be conducted using a more diverse sample at different institutions in Turkey, including public and private universities, in order to generalize these initial findings. However, the results of this study may at least provide a solid foundation for promoting an information literacy initiative at Istanbul University.

Acknowledgments. The research reported in this paper was funded by the Research Fund of Istanbul University (34890). I am thankful to the participating students who willingly took part in this study. I am also grateful to the faculty, staff and librarians of Istanbul University for cooperating me in the course of my study.

References

1. Joint Information System Committee (JISC): User Behaviour Observational Study: User Behaviour in Resource Discovery. Final Report (2009), http://www.jisc.ac.uk/publications/
2. Project Information Literacy, http://projectinfolit.org/publications/
3. Head, A.J., Eisenberg, M.B.: Truth Be Told: How College Students Evaluate and Use Information in the Digital Age. Project Information Literacy Progress Report, University of Washington's Information School (2010), http://projectinfolit.org/publications/
4. Head, A.J., Eisenberg, M.B.: Lessons Learned: How College Students Seek Information in the Digital Age. Project Information Literacy First Year Report with Student Survey Findings, University of Washington's Information School (2009), http://projectinfolit.org/publications/
5. George, C.A., Bright, A., Hurlbert, T., Linke, E.C., Clair, G.S., Stein, J.: Scholarly Use of Information: Graduate Students' Information Seeking Behaviour. University Libraries Research. Paper 21 (2006), http://repository.cmu.edu/lib_science/21
6. Martin, J.: The Information Seeking Behavior of Undergraduate Education Majors: Does Library Instruction Play a Role? Evidence Based Library and Information Practice 3(4), 4–17 (2008)
7. İstanbul Üniversitesi: 2009-2012. Üniversite, İstanbul (2012)
8. Perceptions of Libraries, 2010: Context and Community. OCLC Online Computer Library Center, Inc., Dublin, OH (2010)
9. Connaway, L.S., Dickey, T.J.: The Digital Information Seeker: Report of the Findings from Selected OCLC, RIN, and JISC User Behaviour Projects. HEFCE, Bristol, England (2010), http://www.jisc.ac.uk/media/documents/publications/reports/2010/digitalinformationseekerreport.pdf
10. Griffiths, J.R., Brophy, P.: Student Searching Behavior and the Web: Use of Academic Resources and Google. Library Trends 53(4), 539–554 (2005)
11. O'Brien, H.L., Symons, S.: The Information Behaviors and Preferences of Undergraduate Students. Research Strategies 20(4), 409–423 (2005)
12. Bloom, B.S.: Taxonomy of Educational Objectives: The Classification of Educational Goals: Handbook I, Cognitive Domain. McKay, New York (1969)
13. Information Literacy Competency Standards for Higher Education, American Library Association, http://www.ala.org/acrl/sites/ala.org.acrl/files/content/standards/standards.pdf

Students Readiness for E-Learning: An Assessment on Hacettepe University Department of Information Management

Yurdagül Ünal[1], Gülten Alır[2], and İrem Soydal[1]

[1] Department of Information Management, Hacettepe University, Ankara, Turkey
[2] Department of Information Management, Yıldırım Beyazıt University, Ankara, Turkey
{yurdagul,soydal}@hacettepe.edu.tr, galir@ybu.edu.tr

Abstract. Students are one of the key elements during the implementation of e-learning systems within universities. To be able to build solid and effective e-learning systems, it is important to know the level of students' readiness. In this paper, e-learning readiness of the Department of Information Management (DIM) students at Hacettepe University will be investigated. A 39-item e-learning readiness questionnaire (along with some descriptive questions, such as gender and grade-level) that was tested in previous studies was used to obtain the data. The results show that, although some improvements are needed, DIM students are at the expected level of e-learning readiness, in general.

Keywords: E-learning readiness, higher education, students' readiness.

1   Introduction

The concept of e-learning has been discussed in recent years by many institutions and researchers under the topics of "online learning", "distance learning", "distance education", "virtual learning", etc. in Turkey [1], [2], [3]. Although in practice there are some attempts in the universities to develop e-learning programs, the acceptance or readiness of the faculty and students has not been investigated much. It is important to understand the agents that affect the e-learning eco-system in order to create solid e-learning environments.

This study is based on our previous research which revealed the readiness levels of academic staff working at the Faculty of Letters of Hacettepe University [3]. This time the aim is to investigate the readiness levels of the Department of Information Management (DIM) students. Hacettepe University's DIM is one of the largest departments in the Faculty of Letters, with its 311 undergraduate students. According to the results of our former study, the academic staff of the DIM had the highest scores among other departments in the Faculty, in terms of e-learning readiness.

E-learning is particularly important for information science programs of universities, since the discipline evolves rapidly and this change affects the theoretical curriculum as well as the practice [4].

J.N. Gathegi et al. (Eds.): IMCW 2013, CCIS 423, pp. 137–147, 2014.

2   E-Learning Readiness Assessment

The readiness of teachers [3], [5], [6], [7], [8], [9], [10] and learners [11], [12], [13], [14], [15], [16] for e-learning had been discussed in several studies in the last decade. The studies showed that results related to the different aspects of e-learning readiness can vary over time, among institutions or instruments that were used for the assessment.

The results of e-learning readiness assessments, applied to the academic staff of Turkish higher education, reveal some different results similarly to the international literature. For example, according to Akaslan and Law's study [7], teachers working in the higher education institutes associated with the science of electricity in Turkey have confidence and positive attitudes towards e-learning. On the contrary the assessment which was carried out on the Faculty of Letters academic members revealed that the majority of the departments in the Faculty were not ready for e-learning except for the Department of Information Management [3].[1] These results point to the necessity of assessment studies in different disciplines and show that the readiness level varies from institution to institution.

According to the related literature, readiness levels of students can also vary from their grade-levels to the attitudes of teachers who develop and deliver online courses. For example Hung, et. al's study [13] showed that higher grade college students were significantly more ready than the lower grade students. The study also emphasized the teachers' roles in helping to develop self-directed learning and learner-control skills and attitudes among the students. Another study [14], that stressed the effect of teachers in supporting students to adopt e-learning systems, presented the impact of some constructions of Technology Acceptance Model (such as perceived usefulness, perceived ease of use) on students' attitudes, which affected their intention to use e-learning systems.

Akaslan and Law [11] conducted one of the most comprehensive studies on e-learning readiness of university students in Turkey, which was targeted a specific group: students studying electricity-related disciplines. Their model was based on their previous study [7], in which they assessed the readiness of teachers from several Turkish Universities working in the above mentioned discipline, with some added factors that can be viewed as specific for the students (Fig. 1).

Their assessment was conducted with a 78-item questionnaire based on three main factors; readiness, acceptance and training. The results showed that students were "sufficiently ready" for e-learning [11].

---

[1] In this study [3], e-learning readiness of Hacettepe University Faculty of Letters (HUFL) academic staff was tested with a questionnaire of 37 items that measures the perceptions of the participants in terms of Readiness, Acceptance and Training. It was found out that for most of the items there were statistically significant differences among the mean scores of the departments, and the majority of the departments in the Faculty were not ready for e-learning except for the Department of Information Management.

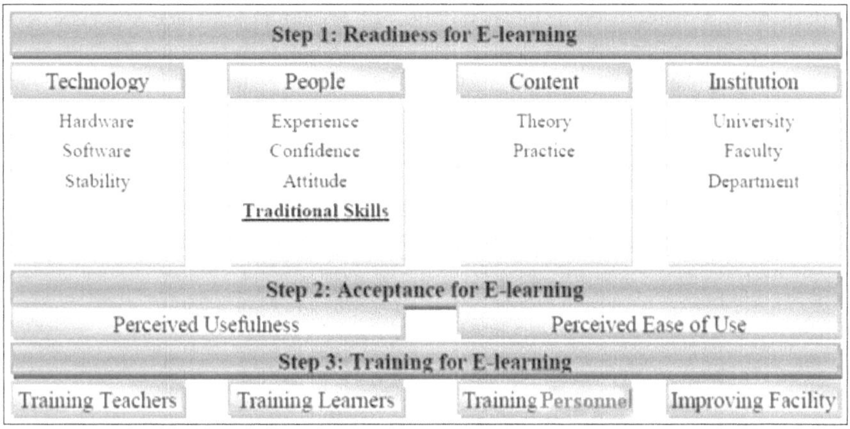

Fig. 1. Akaslan and Law's [11] model for measuring students' readiness for e-learning

Recent studies conducted on students mostly revealed positive results, which mean they generally see themselves almost ready for e-learning [11], [12], [17].

3   Research Methodology

Our previous study [3] revealed that the DIM of Hacettepe University Faculty of Letters is the only department which was almost ready in terms of its academic staff among 16 departments at the Faculty. Starting from this point, we wondered about the situation for DIM students. The aim of this study is to assess the readiness of 311 students who were enrolled in the undergraduate program of DIM at the time this research was conducted. Our paper addresses the following research questions:

- Are the students of DIM ready for e-learning?
- What are the students' perceptions about the main components (availability of technology, use of technology, self confidence, acceptance and training) of e-learning?
- Are there any differences among the students regarding their genders, grade-level and use of smart phones in terms of accepting/rejecting e-learning?

To be able to determine the readiness level, a paper-pen questionnaire was employed to the 311 DIM students. Participants were asked to report their perceptions on readiness for e-learning. The questionnaire had been developed and tested by Akaslan & Law [11] and based on a conceptual model of the readiness for e-learning which assesses the perceived readiness in three phases namely, readiness, acceptance and training (Fig. 1). Original questionnaire had 78 items which are measured with a binary choice or a five-point Likert scale, along with some free text boxes for the participants to explain their scores or choices [11]. Nevertheless, we adopted only the items that can be answered with the Likert scale, in order to understand the basic similarities and differences in the perception of academic staff and students of DIM regarding to e-learning readiness.

Students reported their perceptions on 39 e-learning related items regarding the five main components of e-learning readiness with a five-point Likert scale with 1 being "strongly disagree" and 5 being "strongly agree". Aydın and Taşçı's [18] identification of "expected readiness" for e-learning (which was defined as the mean score of 3.40) was used to interpret the results (see Fig. 2). Same scale was also adopted in the past studies by Akaslan and Law [7], [11] and Soydal, Alır and Ünal [3].

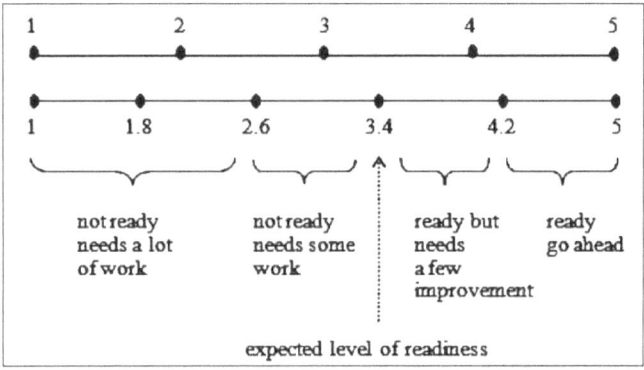

Fig. 2. E-learning readiness assessment model [18]

4   Findings and Discussion

DIM has a four-year undergraduate program and the distribution of the students according to their first to fourth year was; 73, 38, 38 and 129, respectively. There were also 33 students who were not able to graduate and had been studying in DIM for five years or more.

The e-learning readiness survey was applied to all of the DIM undergraduate students and 262 responses were obtained. In other words, our study represents the opinions of 84% of our target audience. The majority of the respondents were female (76%, n= 198[2]) and had personal computers (96%, n= 251). More than half of the respondents had internet-connected smart phones (66%, n=172). There were only six students who stated that they had neither personal computer nor smart phone out of 262 respondents (64%, n=167 of them had both).

The e-learning readiness survey has five main components that aims to reveal "availability of technology" facilities, "use of technology", "self confidence", "acceptance" levels and "training" needs of the respondents. Five-point Likert type scores correspond to strongly disagree/never (1); strongly agree/always (5). Table 1 shows the students' opinions for each item and the overall score for the DIM students in terms of e-learning readiness.

---

[2] This also reflected the total distribution of gender out of 311 undergraduate students of DIM, where 72% (n= 224) of the students were female.

Table 1. Mean scores for the e-learning readiness survey

Description	Items		$\bar{X}$	SD
Availability of Technology	I.1	The hardware facilities are enough.	3.6	1.0
	I.2	The software facilities are enough.	3.4	1.0
	I.3	The speed of the internet access is satisfactory.	2.9	1.1
	I.4	The stability of the internet access is satisfactory.	2.6	1.1
	I.5	I have access to computer whenever I need.	3.6	1.2
	I.6	I can connect internet whenever I need.	3.4	1.1
		Availability of Technology $\bar{X} =$	3.3	1.1
Use of Technology	I.7	I use internet as information source.	4.1	0.7
	I.8	I use e-mail as the main communication tool with my teachers and classmates.	4.0	0.8
	I.9	I use office software (e.g. M.S. PowerPoint, Word, Excel).	4.1	0.8
	I.10	I use social network sites (e.g. Facebook, Twitter).	4.4	0.9
	I.11	I use specific software (e.g. SPSS).	2.6	1.1
	I.12	I use instant messaging (e.g. Google Talk, Skype).	3.5	1.2
	I.13	I use Web 2.0 tools (e.g. Blog, wiki) to share information.	3.2	1.2
	I.14	I use file hosting services (e.g. Google Documents, Dropbox).	3.0	1.2
	I.15	I use learning management systems (e.g. Blackboard, Moodle).	2.6	1.2
	I.16	I use online forums and chat to communicate with my colleagues.	2.9	1.1
	I.17	I use mobile technologies (e.g. Smartphone, Tablet) to connect internet.	3.6	1.3
		Use of Technology $\bar{X} =$	3.5	1.0
Self Confidence	I.18	I have information about what e-learning is.	3.6	0.8
	I.19	I have the skills to operate a computer.	3.9	0.8
	I.20	I am able to use office software for content delivery and demonstration (e.g. M.S. Power Point, Word, Excel).	3.9	0.8
	I.21	I am able to use web browsers (e.g. Internet Explorer, Google Chrome).	4.2	0.7
	I.22	I am able to use search engines (e.g. Google, Yandex).	4.2	0.7
	I.23	I can troubleshoot most problems associated with using a computer.	3.6	0.9

Table 1. (*Continued*)

Table 1. (cont'd)

	I.24	I can use digital file management tools (e.g. deleting or renaming a file on your computer).	4.2	0.8
	I.25	I am able to do my homework by using electronic technology facilities.	4.3	0.8
	I.26	I have enough time to prepare my homework by using electronic technology facilities.	4.1	0.8
	I.27	I am able to use learning management systems (e.g. Blackboard, Moodle).	3.2	1.0
	I.28	I believe that e-learning is easy to use.	3.8	0.9
	I.29	I feel that I am ready for e-learning.	3.8	0.9
		Self Confidence $\bar{X}$ =	3.9	0.8
Acceptance	I.30	I am keen to start e-learning.	3.7	0.9
	I.31	I believe that e-learning can enhance the quality of education.	3.9	0.9
	I.32	I believe that using e-learning can increase my productivity.	3.9	0.9
	I.33	I believe that e-learning is more effectively than the traditional classroom-based approach.	3.6	1.1
	I.34	I believe that e-learning enables learners and instructor to communicate and interact better with one another.	3.5	1.1
	I.35	I believe that e-learning have benefits for education.	3.9	0.9
	I.36	I support implementation of e-learning in my department.	3.9	1.0
		Acceptance $\bar{X}$ =	3.8	1.0
Training	I.37	I need training on e-learning.	4.0	0.8
	I.38	My teachers need training on e-learning.	3.5	1.0
	I.39	My classmates need training on e-learning.	4.0	0.8
		Training $\bar{X}$ =	3.8	0.9
		Overall Mean:	3.6	1.0

Lowest mean scores (Table 1) differ between 2.6 and 3.2, where items are mostly related to *use of technology* and *availability of technology* components. These mean scores can be interpreted as students were not ready when it comes to using specific software (I.11, $\bar{X}$ = 2.6), online forums and chat (I.16, $\bar{X}$ = 2.9), file hosting services (I.14, $\bar{X}$ = 3.0), Web 2.0 tools for information sharing purposes (I.13, $\bar{X}$ = 3.2) and learning management systems (I.15, $\bar{X}$ = 2.6). It seems they were not confident about using learning management systems (I.27, $\bar{X}$ = 3.2) either. Students also did not find stability (I.4, $\bar{X}$ = 2.6) and speed (I.3, $\bar{X}$ = 2.9) of the internet access satisfactory.

Most of the highest mean scores based on the students' perceptions belong to *self confidence* and one of them belongs to *use of technology* component (Table 1). Results show that students were confident about using basic file management tools (I.24, $\bar{X}$ = 4.2), web browsers (I.21, $\bar{X}$ = 4.2), search engines (I.22, $\bar{X}$ = 4.2), social networking sites (I.10, $\bar{X}$ = 4.4) and they were also capable of doing their homework by using the technology (I.25, $\bar{X}$ = 4.3).

It is noteworthy that none of the mean scores for the items regarding e-learning readiness was 5 and the overall mean score (3.6, see Table 1) for the total of 39 items was slightly higher than the expected readiness level, which was indicated by Aydın and Taşçı [18] (see Fig. 2). This result means the students of DIM seems ready for e-learning but there is still some work that needs to be done especially in terms of the availability and the use of technology (Availability of Technology $\bar{X}$ =3.3; Use of Technology $\bar{X}$ =3.5). Moreover, among other components, students seems like they felt themselves "confident" when it comes to e-learning (Self Confidence $\bar{X}$ =3.9) (see Fig. 3).

Fig. 3. Mean scores for e-learning components

With the e-learning readiness survey we also wanted to see the potential differences among the DIM students, in terms of gender, grade-levels and also the use of smart phones, by applying Chi-Square tests.

Gender differences are statistically significant for the Items 8 (I use e-mail as the main communication tool with my teachers and classmates; χ^2= 10.020, p<0.05), 15 (I use learning management systems; χ^2= 10.380, p<0.05), 24 (I can use digital file management tools; χ^2= 11.643, p<0.05) and 33 (I believe that e-learning is more effectively than the traditional classroom-based approach; χ^2= 12.765, p<0.05). In other words, e-mail and some learning management systems usage patterns of the DIM students differ according to their gender, as does using the file management tools on their personal computers. Opinions of DIM students also seem to be differ according to their gender, when it comes to the effectiveness of e-learning as compared to traditional classroom-based learning activities. Females seem more enthusiastic using e-mail, learning management, and file management tools.

E-learning perceptions of the DIM students were also analysed according to their grade levels. Students were asked to indicate the years they spent in the Department as an undergraduate student. According to the results, students' grade-level differences were statistically significant for the items 9 (I use office software; $\chi^2 = 44.892$, $p<0.01$), 10 (I use social network sites; $\chi^2 = 28.904$, $p<0.05$), 11 (I use specific software; $\chi^2 = 54.645$, $p<0.01$), 14 (I use file hosting services; $\chi^2 = 42.348$, $p<0.01$), 28 (I believe that e-learning is easy to use; $\chi^2 = 28.441$, $p<0.05$), 30 (I am keen to start e-learning; $\chi^2 = 28.027$, $p<0.05$), 31 (I believe that e-learning can enhance the quality of education; $\chi^2 = 33.574$, $p<0.01$), 32 (I believe that using e-learning can increase my productivity; $\chi^2 = 35.677$, $p<0.01$), 33 (I believe that e-learning is more effectively than the traditional classroom-based approach; $\chi^2 = 35.129$, $p<0.01$), 34 (I believe that e-learning enables learners and instructor to communicate and interact better with one another; $\chi^2 = 27.491$, $p<0.05$), 35 (I believe that e-learning have benefits for education; $\chi^2 = 44.286$, $p<0.01$), 36 (I support implementation of e-learning in my department; $\chi^2 = 41.514$, $p<0.01$), 37 (I need training on e-learning; $\chi^2 = 34.023$, $p<0.01$), 38 (My teachers need training on e-learning; $\chi^2 = 37.626$, $p<0.01$) and 39 (My classmates need training on e-learning; $\chi^2 = 33.696$, $p<0.01$). These items showed that students' grade-level affected their opinions especially for the *use of technology*, *acceptance* and *training*-related issues. Their tendency to accept e-learning grew as the number of years they spent in the Department increased. Moreover, they seemed more confident while using technology as their grade-levels rose. On the other hand, regarding the need for training, first, second and third year students seemed relatively more enthusiastic for e-learning training, possibly because of their awareness of lack of information about the topic.

We also tried to find out if there were any differences among the e-learning perceptions of DIM students in terms of their use of smart phones. The students were asked if they had an internet-connected smart phone and 66% of them answered that they did. The results showed that the smart phone user and non-user students' opinions differ for the items 4 (The stability of the internet access is satisfactory; $\chi^2 = 11.337$, $p<0.05$), 5 (I have access to computer whenever I need; $\chi^2 = 9.968$, $p<0.05$), 6 (I can connect internet whenever I need; $\chi^2 = 11.976$, $p<0.05$), 10 (I use social network sites; $\chi^2 = 13.978$, $p<0.01$), 12 (I use instant messaging; $\chi^2 = 20.096$, $p<0.01$), 14 (I use file hosting services; $\chi^2 = 9.530$, $p<0.05$), 17 (I use mobile technologies to connect internet; $\chi^2 = 108.514$, $p<0.01$) and 36 (I support implementation of e-learning in my department; $\chi^2 = 14.978$, $p<0.01$). These results indicated that students' opinions for some items of the *availability of technology* and *use of technology* components and also one item for *acceptance* were affected by the students' smart phone usage habits. The ones that were using internet-connected smart phones seemed more ready in terms of adopting technology, which was one of the core elements of e-learning.

5   Conclusion

E-learning is one of the hot topics, especially for universities' agendas. For an effective implementation of an e-learning programme some serious planning and analysis need to be done. Assessing teachers' and students' readiness for e-learning is one of the main factors during the planning and implementation of e-learning projects.

According to our previous study, teaching staff of DIM was the most ready department within the 16 departments of the Faculty of Letters of Hacettepe University [3]. In this study we tried to assess DIM students' e-learning readiness.

Based on the Aydın and Taşçı's [18] assessment interpretation (see Fig. 2) the results showed that, although the students of DIM were not fully ready to adopt e-learning, for the "use of technology", "self confidence", "acceptance" and "training" related issues, they were slightly higher than the expected level of readiness. This can be interpreted to mean that the students of DIM were ready but some improvements need to be done. Developing training programs for the students in order to help them to understand e-learning better, making its benefits more clear, offering better internet infrastructures with more computer and mobile technology facilities can help students increase their readiness levels. The only component below the expected level of readiness was "availability of technology". This means, before implementing any kind of e-learning programs, students' technological facilities must be improved. This is also interesting, because almost all students (96%) declare that they have personal computers and more than half of them (66%) said that they have Internet-connected smart phones. This makes us think that, students might not be satisfied with the technological facilities that they assume the university has to offer them.

Gender, grade-level and smart-phone usage differences also had some effect on some items related to e-learning-readiness. Although females seem more enthusiastic about using e-mail, learning management and file management tools, these clues about the opinion differences between the genders and their possible causes should be analyzed more and examined with some in-depth research. On the other hand, results also showed that opinions on the *use of technology*, *acceptance* and *training*-related issues may vary according to the students' grade-levels. Fourth-year students seemed especially more adapted to e-learning and its components. Moreover, the results indicated that first, second and third-year students need to be trained more about e-learning. Since DIM has a technology-based curriculum, it could be viewed as normal for senior students to get used to technology and more readily adopt e-learning related issues. Furthermore, the use of internet-connected smart phones also affected students' perceptions regarding the *availability* and *use of technology* components. They seem more open to mobile technologies and probably wished to stay connected from anywhere/anytime, which is also important for competent e-learning activities.

Although the findings of this study may give some tips about the profile of the students of a department with a technology based curriculum, more comprehensive studies must be conducted and reported throughout Turkey in order to determine a model for a course of action for transitioning to an e-learning system in the whole country.

References

1. Baltacı-Goktalay, S., Ocak, M.A.: Faculty Adoption of Online Technology in Higher Education. The Turkish Online Journal of Educational Technology 5, 37–43 (2006)
2. Koçer, H.E.: Web Tabanlı Uzaktan Eğitim. Unpublished master's thesis, Selçuk University, Konya (2001)
3. Soydal, İ., Alır, G., Ünal, Y.: Are Turkish Universities Ready for E-learning: A Case of Hacettepe University Faculty of Letters. Information Services & Use 31, 281–291 (2011)
4. Roknuzzaman, M.D., Umemoto, K.: Knowledge Management Education in Library and Information Science Schools: An Exploratory Study. In: Asia-Pacific Conference on Library & Information Education & Practice, Preparing Information Professionals for International Collaboration, Tsukuba, Japan, March 6-8 (2009)
5. Hegarty, B., Perman, M.: Approaches and Implications of eLearning Adoption in Relation to Academic Staff Efficacy and Working Practice Final Report, Universal College of Learning (2005), http://cms.steo.govt.nz/NR/rdonlyres/8C221A73-CF28-4CC9-83E8-B8FD7D9C1164/0/ALETfinalReport251006.pdf
6. Bonanno, P.: Developing an Instrument to Assess Teachers' Readiness for Technology-Enhanced Learning. In: 14th International Conference on Interactive Collaborative Learning (ICL 2011), Piešťany, Slovakia, September 21-23, pp. 21–23 (2011)
7. Akaslan, D., Law, E.L.-C.: Measuring Teachers' Readiness for E-learning in Higher Education Institutions Associated with the Subject of Electricity in Turkey. In: Proceedings of 2011 IEEE Global Engineering Education Conference (EDUCON)-Learning Environments and Ecosystems in Engineering Education, Amman, Jordan, pp. 481–490 (2010)
8. Tezer, M., Bicen, H.: Üniversite Öğretim Elemanlarinin E-eğitim Sistemlerine Yönelik Hazır Bulunuşluğu. In: International Educational Technology Conference, Anadolu University, Turkey (2008)
9. So, K.K.T.: The E-learning Readiness of Teachers in Hong Kong. In: Proceedings of the Fifth IEEE International Conference on Advanced Learning Technologies (ICALT 2005), pp. 806–808. IEEE Computer Society, Washington, DC (2005)
10. Kaur, K., Abas, Z.W.: An Assessment of E-learning Readiness at Open University Malaysia. In: Proceedings of the International Conference on Computers in Education (ICCE), Melbourne, Australia, November 30-December 4 (2004)
11. Akaslan, D., Law, E.L.-C.: Measuring Student E-Learning Readiness: A Case about the Subject of Electricity in Higher Education Institutions in Turkey. In: Leung, H., Popescu, E., Cao, Y., Lau, R.W.H., Nejdl, W. (eds.) ICWL 2011. LNCS, vol. 7048, pp. 209–218. Springer, Heidelberg (2011)
12. Tubaishat, A., Lansari, A.: Are Students Ready to Adopt E-learning? A Preliminary E-readiness Study of a University in the Gulf Region. International Journal of Information and Communication Technology Research 1, 210–215 (2011)
13. Hung, M.L., Chou, C., Chen, C.H., Own, Z.Y.: Learner Readiness for Online Learning: Scale Development and Student Perceptions. Computers & Education 55, 1080–1090 (2010)
14. Park, S.Y.: An Analysis of the Technology Acceptance Model in Understanding University Students' Behavioral Intention to Use E-learning. Educational Technology & Society 12, 150–162 (2009)

15. Jahng, N., Krug, D., Zhang, Z.: Student Achievement in Online Distance Education Compared to Face-to-face Education. European Journal of Open, Distance and E-Learning (2007), `http://www.eurodl.org/materials/contrib/2007/Jahng_Krug_Zhang.htm`
16. Smith, P.J., Murphy, K.L., Mahoney, S.E.: Towards Identifying Factors Underlying Readiness for Online Learning: An Exploratory Study. Distance Education 24, 57–67 (2003)
17. Moftakhari, M.M.: Evaluating E-learning Readiness of Faculty of Letters of Hacettepe. Unpublished master's thesis, Hacettepe University, Ankara (2013)
18. Aydın, C.H., Taşçı, D.: Measuring Readiness for E-learning: Reflections from an Emerging Country. Educational Technology and Society 8, 244–257 (2005)

Evaluation of Scientific Disciplines in Turkey: A Citation Analysis Study

Zehra Taşkın and Güleda Doğan

Hacettepe University, Department of Information Management, 06800, Ankara, Turkey
{ztaskin,gduzyol}@hacettepe.edu.tr

Abstract. This study focuses on Turkish scholars' information use. Using citation analysis, it investigates a total of 197,687 publications in our main scientific disciplines (pure sciences, engineering, social sciences and arts & humanities) extracted from Web of Science (1928-2009). Authors (at least one of them) of these publications were all affiliated with Turkish institutions. Differences between these disciplines and between their sub-disciplines in terms of average author number, multiple authorship, half-life, publication types, journals characteristics were determined. Findings of this study can be helpful for national-level policy making on scientific productivity that will help Turkish scholarship to reach international level.

Keywords: Information behavior, Turkish scholars, scientific disciplines, pure sciences, social sciences, engineering, arts and humanities.

1   Introduction

Each individual from any working area or academic discipline retrieves, analyzes, and synthesizes information in different ways. Consequently, it is important to understand information behaviors of individuals, groups or disciplines. Information behaviors can be identified by using surveys or questionnaires. Additionally, it is also possible to evaluate publications and citations with the aim of revealing behaviors.

Information behaviors in specific disciplines are the subject of many studies in the literature. These studies concentrated on pure scientists and engineers at the beginning. After the Second World War ended, controlling material production by scientists and engineers became vital for countries [1]. Thus, the first information behavior studies written in these years were for scientists and engineers. Even Wilson claimed that "the study of information-seeking behavior can be said to be the study of scientists' information-seeking behavior" in that period [2]. Studies on social scientists began with INFROSS project in 1967 at Bath University [3]. At last, the studies focused on the people working in the arts and humanities fields. Therefore, it is possible to say that understanding people's information needs and behaviors has become important to customize information services according to people's needs.

The main aim of this study is to evaluate the scientific disciplines comprising of the pure sciences, engineering, social sciences and art & humanities in Turkey by

J.N. Gathegi et al. (Eds.): IMCW 2013, CCIS 423, pp. 148–155, 2014.
© Springer-Verlag Berlin Heidelberg 2014

using citation analysis. It is also aimed to reveal differences in scientific disciplines and sub-disciplines. To achieve these aims, Turkey-addressed publications placed in *Web of Science* were analyzed.

2   Research Questions and Methodology

This paper seeks answers to the following research questions;

- Do the publication types differ for each discipline?
- Are there any differences between disciplines and sub-disciplines in terms of average number of authors for each publication?
- Are there any differences between disciplines and sub-disciplines with regard to single/multiple authorship?
- What is the citation half-life of publications in terms of their disciplines? Are there any differences among disciplines and sub-disciplines?
- Which journals do the authors choose to publish in? Are the authors discriminating to choose high-impact journals?
- What are the mostly cited journals and their impacts for each discipline? Is it possible to draw a parallel between selected journals for publication and mostly cited journals?

To answer these questions, 197,687 Turkey-addressed publications placed in *Web of Science* between 1928 and 2009 were gathered. Data about authors, journals, affiliations and countries were unified for the aim of accessing accurate data. Then, data was divided into disciplines and sub-disciplines by using *Web of Science* subject categories. Four different disciplines were determined for general comparisons: pure sciences, social sciences, engineering and art & humanities. Furthermore, the following were determined to be sub-disciplines: physics, chemistry, biology and mathematics for pure sciences; history, economy, library and information science and education for social sciences; chemical engineering, computer engineering, electrical and electronic engineering for engineering; art, philosophy and humanities for arts and humanities. 54,242 pure sciences, 2,846 social sciences, 11,042 engineering and 316 arts and humanities. Publications were closely evaluated to find out differences between these disciplines.

Unfortunately, it is impossible to avoid inequality in the data on *Web of Science* because of the distribution of journals in the disciplines. For example, there were 54,242 Turkey-addressed pure sciences publications indexed in *Web of Science* as compared with only 316 in the arts and humanities. Also, because of the nature of the content in the *Web of Science*, it was not surprising to that the most produced publication type was articles. 77.2% of the documents produced by Turkey between 1928 and 2009 were found to be articles [4]. The main limitation for this study is quantitative differences between disciplines and the content of *Web of Science*. To avoid the limitation, each discipline was evaluated within itself and percentages were emphasized. Also, instead of just articles, different types of publications were also considered when comparing publication types for disciplines.

3   Findings and Discussion

3.1   Publications and their Distribution by Year

Fig. 1 shows the graph of annual percent of distribution of publications for Turkey for each discipline.

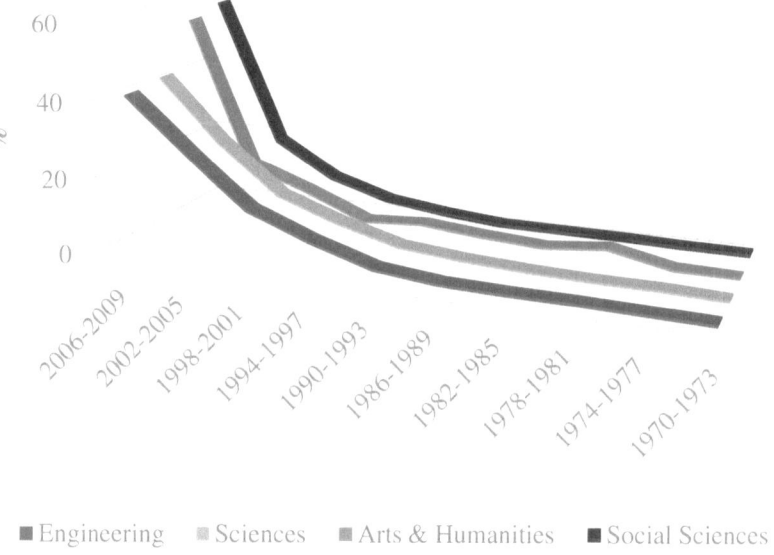

■ Engineering   ■ Sciences   ■ Arts & Humanities   ■ Social Sciences

Fig. 1. Publication count for each discipline for Turkey

Publication counts have increased since 1980s. Publication counts on each discipline approximately doubled during each 4-year-period after the year 2000. This situation can be explained by two factors: the founding of The Council of Higher Education in 1981 [5] and the regional development policy of citation indexes [6]. The number of Turkish journals in *Web of Science* has grown considerably with the introduction of the regional development policy.

3.2   Document Types

Document types provide tips for understanding information usage of disciplines. However, research conducted by using citation databases generally reveals that the most produced documents are articles. The reason for this kind of findings is the content of the citation databases which generally include mainly journals. Unsurprisingly, the mostly produced document type for Turkish scientific disciplines is articles at 83.7% for science; 89.7% for engineering; 78.1% for social sciences, and 79.4% for arts and humanities. Letters, notes and reviews are also produced for all the disciplines. Meeting abstracts are mostly written for the field of science and engineering. Book reviews, biographical items and art exhibit reviews are in the arts and humanities field. The findings are important to show variety of document types and their distribution.

3.3   Number of Authors

Co-authorship can be regarded as an indicator of team work and scientific communication. According to our study, scholars who work in the arts and humanities discipline prefer working alone. Maximum author count for arts and humanities literature is 10. Social sciences and engineering resemble each other from the point of co-authorship. Maximum author count for engineering is 101 (electrical-electronic engineering), for social sciences 105 (psychology). The median of author number for each publication is 2 for both disciplines. Science discipline is different from other areas. Biology authors give preference to working together (median is 4). Maximum author count is 105 for biology, 2010 for physics, 40 for chemistry and 10 for mathematics. Mathematics discipline is approaching social sciences author numbers. Information about co-authorship is shown on Fig. 2.

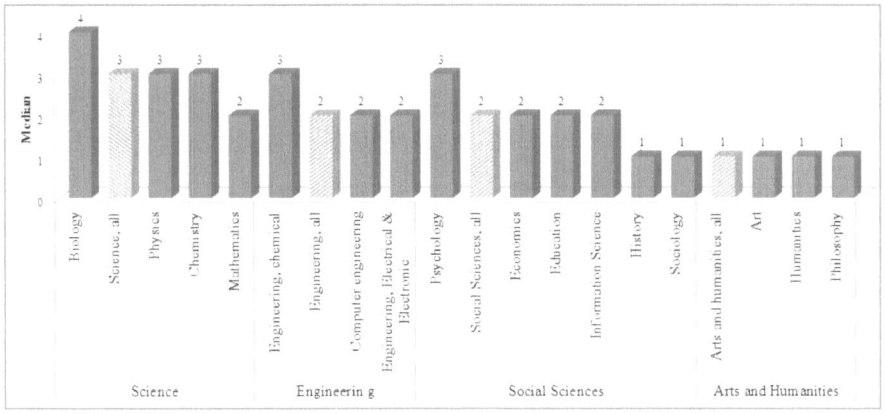

Fig. 2. Median number of authors for different disciplines

Findings of this study bear out earlier studies. According to a 2009 [7], single authorship is prevalent in social sciences (78%) and arts and humanities (93%). This study found that multiple authorship is preferred for engineering (62%) and sciences (64%) disciplines. The findings regarding single and multiple authorships of Turkish scholars according to disciplines is shown in Fig. 3.

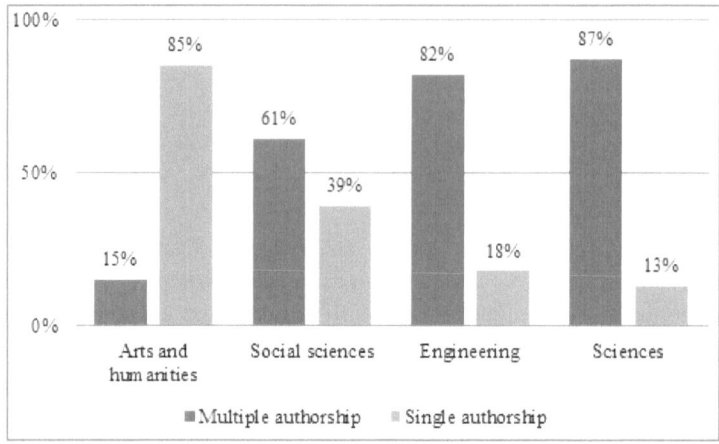

Fig. 3. Single and multiple authorships of Turkish scholars

3.4   Literature Obsolescence and Citing Half-Lives

Scientific publications are cited less and less as the years pass. Therefore, we need to calculate half-lives to understand citation potentials of publications. Half-life is defined in the literature as "the median age of an article that were cited or citing" [8], [9]. Thomson Reuters defines citing half-life as "the median age of articles cited by the journal in the *JCR* year" [10]. Fig. 4 shows the half-lives of the citations calculated for this study, according to disciplines.

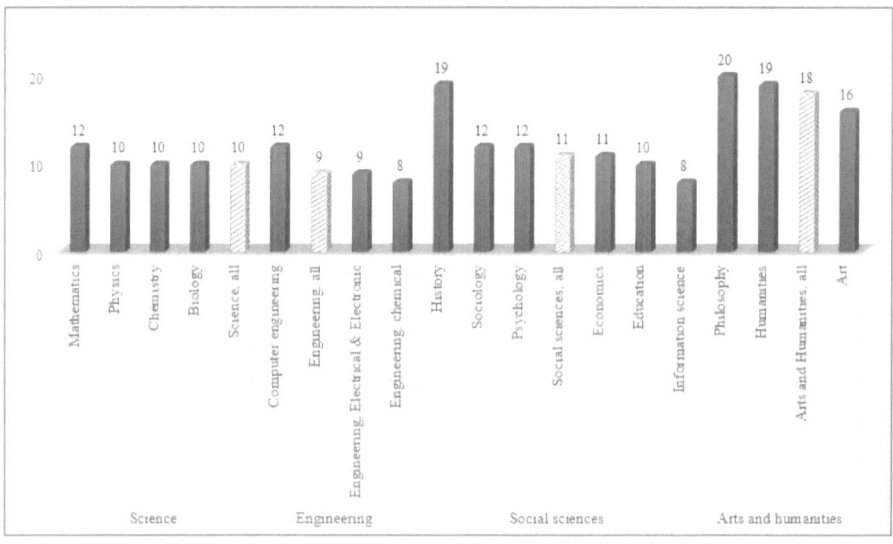

Fig. 4. Half-lives

Our study identified philosophy and history as having the slowest half-life. Mathematics, history, art, information science and computer engineering areas show different characteristics with respect to their major areas.

3.5   Journal Choices of Authors

Information about journal choices of authors may be helpful to understand research trends of each discipline. Education, physics and computer engineering sub-disciplines, which reflect the characteristics of their disciplines' features, were chosen for journal choices evaluation in the context of this study. *Journal Citation Reports* (*JCR*) 2012 edition was used as a data tool.

Turkish journals which are indexed in *Web of Science* generally have been chosen for publication by Turkish education scholars. It seems that impact factor is not an important determiner for choices. Table 1 shows the mostly preferred and the top journals in the education field.

Table 1. Top and mostly preferred journals of education field

Top journals	IF*	JR**	NTP***
Review of Educational Research	4.229	1	0
Learning and Instruction	3.337	2	3
American Educational Research Journal	3.104	3	0
Journal of The Learning Sciences	3.036	4	2
Academy of Management Learning & Education	3.000	5	0
Preferred Journals	**IF***	**JR***	**NTP***
Hacettepe Universitesi Egitim Fakultesi Dergisi	0.350	173	141
Kuram ve Uygulamada Egitim Bilimleri	0.316	179	124
Egitim Arastirmalari-Eurasian Journal of Educational Research	0.455	142	123
Egitim ve Bilim-Education and Science	0.429	150	113
Turkish Online Journal of Educational Technology	n/a	n/a	46

*IF: Impact factor
**JR: Journal rank in the category
***NTP: Number of Turkey-addressed publications

The five mostly preferred journals are published in Turkey. However, Turkish scholars on education field published only five articles in top journals of *JCR*. It shows that locality of journals is more important factor than impact factors in education and social sciences field.

The criterion for journal selection for physics seems to be different from education. Impact factor is not an identifier of journal selection for Turkish physics scholars, however, they have not preferred Turkish journals. Table 2 shows the selections of the physics scholars.

Table 2. Top and mostly preferred journals of physics field

Top Journals	IF*	JR**	NTP***
Reviews of Modern Physics	44.982	1	1
Nature Materials	35.749	1	4
Advances In Physics	34.294	2	1
Nature Photonics	27.254	2	0
Physics Reports-Review Section of Physics Letters	22.929	2	3
Preferred Journals	**IF***	**JR***	**NTP***
Acta Crystallographica Section E-Structure Reports Online	n/a	n/a	923
Energy Conversion and Management	2.775	4	449
Physical Review B	3.767	15	381
Acta Crystallographica Section C-Crystal Structure Communications	0.492	21	352
Journal of Sound and Vibration	1.613	10	318

*IF: Impact factor
**JR: Journal rank in the category
***NTP: Number of Turkey-addressed publications in this journal

Computer engineering field was evaluated by its journal choices. Similarly to physics scholars, impact factors are also insignificant for computer engineers. Table 3 shows the situation for computer engineering field.

Table 3. Top and mostly preferred journals of computer engineering field

Top journals	IF*	JR**	NTP***
ACM Transactions on Graphics	3.361	1	1
SIAM Journal of Imaging Sciences	2.966	2	0
IEEE Transactions on Software Engineering	2.588	3	5
Communications of the ACM	2.511	4	7
IEEE Transactions on Services Computing	2.460	5	0
Preferred Journals	**IF***	**JR***	**NTP***
Mathematical and Computer Modelling	1.420	26	83
Advances in Engineering Software	1.220	35	65
Simulation Modelling Practice and Theory	1.159	40	26
Mathematics and Computers in Simulation	0.836	64	19
Journal of Systems and Software	1.135	41	16

*IF: Impact factor
**JR: Journal rank in the category
***NTP: Number of Turkey-addressed publications in this journal

Journal information about Arts and Humanities field could not be collected for this study because of the non-existence of a *JCR* collection for *A&HCI*. We suggest that the journal selection criteria of scholars in this field should be evaluated closely in accordance with our results for other disciplines presented in Table 1, 2 and 3. Although journal choices will depend the characteristics of the specific discipline, it is important to reveal other reasons for all disciplines. In this way, it may be possible to update the national incentive system in the context of journal selection criteria.

4   Results and Evaluation

This study aimed to reveal the information use of Turkish scholars based on Turkey-addressed *Web of Science* publications for four main fields: pure sciences, engineering, social sciences, arts and humanities. Findings show that the article is the most preferred document type for these four fields, although, due to the structure of *Web of Science*, this finding should not be generalized. Co-authorship is most common for engineering and science, especially among biologists. Mathematicians have the lowest rate of co-authorship among scientists. Arts and humanities have the highest rate of single authorship. Half-life is the highest for arts and humanities in general. Information science is closer to engineering in terms of half-life. Turkish scholars prefer Turkey-addressed journals for publishing their papers; impact factor is not the determining factor for their choices. Findings of this study reinforce the findings of similar studies in the literature and can be used for scientific and financial decisions of universities and research institutions.

References

1. Price, D.D.S.: Little Science, Big Science. Columbia University Press, New York (1963)
2. Wilson, T.D.: The Cognitive Approach to Information-Seeking Behavior and Information Use. Social Science Information Studies 4, 197–204 (1984)
3. Line, M.: The Information Uses and Needs of Social Scientists: An Overview of INFROSS. Aslib Proceedings 23, 412–434 (1971)
4. Al, U., Sezen, U., Soydal, İ.: Türkiye'nin Bilimsel Yayınlarının Sosyal Ağ Analizi Yöntemiyle Değerlendirilmesi [The Evaluation of Scientific Publications of Turkey Using Social Network Analysis Method]. TÜBİTAK Social Sciences and Humanities Research Group - Project No: SOBAG 110K044, Ankara (2012)
5. The Council of Higher Education: Tarihçe [History]. (n.d.), http://www.yok.gov.tr/web/guest/tarihce
6. Testa, J.: Regional Content Expansion Update: Web of Science 5.0 (2008), http://wokinfo.com/media/pdf/RExEssay.pdf
7. Uçak, N., Al, U.: The Differences Among Disciplines in Scholarly Communication: A Bibliometric Analysis of Theses. Libri 59, 166–179 (2009)
8. Tonta, Y.: Türk Kütüphaneciliği Dergisi, 1987-2001 [Journal of Turkish Librarianship, 1987-2001]. Türk Kütüphaneciliği 16, 282–320 (2002)
9. Earle, P., Vickery, B.: Social Science Literature Use in the UK as Indicated by Citations. Journal of Documentation 25, 123–141 (1969)
10. Reuters, T.: Cited Half Life (2012), http://admin-apps.webofknowledge.com/JCR/help/h_ctghl.htm#jcrnlc

Author Index